WALKING IN FAITH AS A REBORN CHRISTIAN

Philip L. Royse II

WESTBOW®
PRESS
A DIVISION OF THOMAS NELSON
& ZONDERVAN

WestBow Press books may be ordered through booksellers or by contacting:

WestBow Press
A Division of Thomas Nelson & Zondervan
1663 Liberty Drive
Bloomington, IN 47403
www.westbowpress.com
1 (866) 928-1240

ISBN: 978-1-4908-4490-9 (sc)

Library of Congress Control Number: 2014912742

Printed in the United States of America.

WestBow Press rev. date: 12/17/2014

Intro.

My name is Philip L. Royse II I grew up in a little town in New Richmond Ohio. When I was 42 I owned my own business and drinking and drugs was a way of life for me. My father had become a Christian 2 years prior to this time and was faithful to his church. He would visit me at my place of business and ask me to go to church with him. My answer was always I believe in God but I don't need church. My father was very patient with me and would say I love you anyway.

One day my father came to me and asked if I would got to church to see him and my mother renew their wedding vows. I said yes I will go to church for that. That day Jesus came into my life and I haven't been the same since. Then 2 months later I began to write this book every morning for 2 hours before I would go to work it took me 3 years to complete it. After 5 years I became a reverend at New Beginnings Church and still attend there today. The people I help the most are the ones that were just like me.

One thing I know is God chose me and set me free from my destructive ways The biggest lie I ever told was I don't need church. The Lord said he is my shepard and I shall not want and he would never leave me or forsake me. He said my seed shall not beg for bread and by his stripes I am healed. I pray if this book helps just one person then everything I endured was worth it all. God bless!

In nineteen fourty three a boy was born in Flemmingburg Kentucky he lived thier with his mother and father untill he was twelve and his mother & father would move to New Richmond, Ohio where he would go to school and meet his High School sweet heart and after they graduated they would get married and he would become a truck driver to support him and his wife he drove all over the United States and he would take big pride in what he was doing and he would strive to be the best, this just was his attitude, he really believed in doing the best job possible, and he and his wife would start their own family in nineteen sixty one his wife would give birth to their first born which was a little boy and they name the baby after him, and almost the same day the first little boy was born she would give birth to another little boy they were just two days from being a year apart and as the boys were growing up everyone would think they were twins they looked alot alike and they were about the same size. Now since this man was a truck driver he would move around a lot from state to state were ever this man would get his best job offer, could you imagine back in the early sixties how hard it must have been moving from place to place trying and trying to raise two boys. His wife could get little help from her family. You know her job raising two boys in the sixties was not easy, seeing how her husband was a truck driver and he was on the road alot sometimes for weeks at a time so this would mean that the wife would have to tend to the two boys and if I had to guess I would say she had her hands full, but she loved this man and her two boys and she would do what ever it took to take care of her three men. As time would go on his wife had given birth to a girl and they moved back to New Richmond, Ohio, and her husband was still truck driving and the boy's would start school their and his wife could get a little help from their family's, and as the time went on we are now going into nineteen seventy and his wife would give birth to their fourth child which was another little girl now by this time the man and his wife would decide that they need to stay put for the children and the mans father in law would sell him a Tavern in New Richmond and they decided to run the business themselves. He began to drink a lot of alcohol, and the wife would be running the Tavren almost by herself and this would take a toll on the marriage and it would get so bad that the man would begin hitting his wife and she would end up leaving him and then the man would end up drinking even more and more. By this time the boy's were about fifteen and sixteen the two girls went with their mother and the two boy's stayed with their dad. Now if you could imagen a fifteen and a sixteen year old boy's staying with their father who own a Tavern and they lived over top of the Tavren and this Tavren was open from about ten am to one pm well let say this the dad really didn't have much time for the boy's they would do pretty much what they wanted to do. They would begin to run the streets and they would steal beer from their dads Tavren and money and they would buy pot with the money the boy's would really take a turn for the worst but their dad would really not notice untill the boy's would start getting in trouble and the boy's had went to their Grandparents house for the weeken and they stoled their car and run away the boy's were gone about two weeks they had wrecked their grandparents car and it was a few days after that they would get caught my the police, now this would probaly be the best thing that would happen to the boy's because their dad and the police would come up with a choice for the boy's they could go to jail or they could go to Job Corps and the boy's would chose Job Corps which was in Oregon that was twenty six miles up a mountain and this would change these two boy's arround for the good and if I had to say this was the wake up call that they needed, and it would even help the dad, because he would become proud of his two son's for getting it together and doing good in Oregon they would often write him and send awards back to their father that they had earn. But betime the boys had got back their dad was still drinking alot, and he had lost alot of weight he had went from two hundred and twenty pounds to one hundred and twenty pounds it was bad not only that but the dad was going to have to sell the bussiness to pay all his debts but it would work out the dad would sell and pay his debts and him and the oldest son would get jobs at a power plant as welders because that was what his son learn in Job Corps. Now this would help the man alot he never quit drinking but he was not drinking as much. Then a few years later their father would meet a woman and marrie her, at this time their mother was allready remarried and by now their girls are ten and fifteen and their mother would give birth to another little girl in nineteen eighty. They all still lived in New Richmond and not far from one and another two years has went by and alot has went on the mother and her husband had decided to get a divorce and the father also was getting a divorce. I believe what happens next was meant to be because the mother and father began to talk and would get remarried and he would adopt the daughter as his own. And they would become very close to one and another he was close to the other children too especially the fourth child because they spent alot of time together. Now they was all back together as a family, and living their lives, for the next five year's. When traggedy would hit their family, their dad would have a heart attack at the age of fourty five. He would need surgery the doctor said: he would have to do a five way by pass and that he was going to take a vain out of his leg and use it to repair the one's going to his heart. The family was devstated, and was afraid that they might lose him. For this hospital told the family this would be the largest by pass surgery formed at this time here. Then after the surgry the doctor would come out and talk to the family and tell them that their father had been through alot, but that he was a fighter, and that he was doing good for what he had been through. So the family felt relieved in what the doctor had told them. But what they didn't know is how this would change the man's life. You see the man would have to make changes, he would quit smoking, and he would go on a diet that the doctor would put him on and it was like a miracle the man was getting better each day, and it was not long before the man would get to come home, it was like a new start for him.

So as their lives went on, it would come to the year ninteen ninty five and this man was running a trucking company, and they were closing down his location and moving. This man had a choice to be laid off or to go back as a truck driver. So he would talk it over with his wife and he would decide to drive again. For after all it was his passion, and he just enjoyed doing it, and at this time all his children was growed up and starting their own families, except the last little girl which was fifteen, and doing very well in school and her activitys. So he would be on the road again doing what he loved, besides fishing he loved to get his buddies and just go fishing. So everytime I would see this man he was allways happy and content with how his life was going. He was truck driving and fishing and working on old car's and building different things arround the house and it was now ninteen ninty eight and his last child was getting ready to graduate from High School and was talking about college to him she want to be a school teacher, and he was proud of her, so life was good for this man. But as his life would go on we would come into the year two thousand and two and he was leaving for a track run. We must remember this family had been through so much good and bad times but some how they allways stuck together, and no one would know what was about to happen next it is August two thousand and two, and he was on his way home from Indianapolis when tragedy would strike again. As the man was driving he began to get pains in his stomach, and he told me the further he drove the more the pain grew, and that it got to ware he could hardly stand the pain. So he had a pillow in his sleeper, so he put it between him and the steering wheel of his truck, and he told me that he stayed hunched over the steering wheel till he got home. After he was home the pain was so bad that his family took him to the hospital, and by now he was having a real hard time even to with stand the pain. When he got their a doctor began examine him and the doctor knew right away that it was very bad and that the man had cancer, and that he would have to operate as soon as possible the man didn't even have to think about it he agreed with the doctor, and gave the doctor the ok for the operation. So the doctor set the operation for the next morning. When the operation was over the doctor told his wife and their children, that he had done all he could do, and that it was so bad that he had to remove the man's whole colon, and the doctor said: that the colon was so destroyed it was falling through his fingers as he was trying to remove it, and that he would have to wash, and clean out his body with a cleaning fluid, and that he hoped, he got all of the poison out of his body, then he said: this man has been through so much, and it is real bad and that if he would make it past three hours he would be very lucky. So then the family began hurting, and crying and was afraid that their father was about to die this time for shore. As they set their one of his daughters had called her pastor, and he was on his way. Now when the Pastor had arrived he came in the mans hospital room. The Pastor began talking to the man, and the Pastor could see the fear in the mans eyes, and he asked, if he could pray for him, and if he wanted to bring Jesus into his heart, and if he would accept Jesus as his Lord and Saviour, and the man said yes and tell God if he will give me one more year, I will get it right for God. So the pastor praid to God for this man, and the family was cring and praying too. Now as they all sat in their fathers room just watching the clock the father said I'am not realy in anymore pain like I was before the operation, and the man was laying in his hospital bed talking and telling his family that everthing was going to be ok, and he would just smile. Now as the clock came to the third hour the doctor came back to the mans hospital room to examinen him and when the doctor was done he said, the man appears to be a little better but, that he couldn't explain it. Then the doctor told the family that he didn't think the man would make it past three days. So the family was still very hurt, and sad, because the doctor had only give the man three days to live so they all stayed at the hospital for three days, but as the family stayed their they could see that the man was getting a little better each day. Now when the third day came. The doctor examine the man, and he said, I cannot explain why he is still alive, because this man has been through so much. I had to take out his whole colon and I had to sow his vowels to his small intestents, and I believe he needs to enjoy what time he has left and just try to make him as comfortable as you can. Because he will only have about three months at most to live. But what everyone else was seeing, was everytime someone came into his hospital room he would be smiling, and he would be polite, and would tell them don't feal sorry for me. Because the things that I have done in my life has caused all this, and I have excepted the responsibility of what has happen to me, but I will not give up now, and it will be ok. Now it has been one week and you could see that this man was just about to start to fight for his life, because it has been only seven days, and the man was eating and drinking what ever he wanted, and when any of the nurses or doctor would check on him, they would say, I cannot beleive how well you are doing, and that you are still with us and you are allways in good cheer, and the family would just smile, because seven days ago they feared that they was going to lose him, and they still didn't know how much longer he would have, but it sure seemed a little better, because he was doing a little more each day and he was talking and laughing with who ever came to visit with him, and that was alot, because this man was well liked and he had a good size family, and now it has been two weeks and when the doctor came into the room he told the man, if you feal able to go home you may. Now this is the same doctor that said, he would be lucky for three hours, and that he might make it three days, and then when the man made it past that time the doctor then gave the man three months, and now it is two weeks later and this same doctor is now releasing the man to go home and the man just smiled and said ok.

This mans two daughters and their mother went to the same church and the other daughter went to a church in South Carolina, and his two son's had not been to church sense they where young boys, and they are fourty one and fourty two, and now that the man was out of the hospital he kept to his commitment, and joined his wifes and his two daughters church, and as this man devoted his life to God, and Jesus and he and the pastor of this church would became such good friends that the pastor told me that this man was more like a father to him. The pastor also told me that he had a father, but that he had a drinking promble and that he was mean to the children, but that he still loved his dad and that his dad did come to the Lord and that he past on to be with the Lord, and then the pastor said; that this man he prayed for back in August 2002 was more than just a friend, that he was more like a father to him, and what happens next is a story all of it's own. This mans wife told me that her husband and her pastor would begin to be with each other everyday, and that if they was not golfing they would travel to Lake Erie where the mans second house was and his boat was right on the lake shore. She also said that he would save every fish that he caught, and then she said that it had been past the three months that the doctor had given her husband and that he was beating all the odds that the doctor's gave him, and that the doctor could not explain why he was still alive, and that her husband could start chemo. in a couple of months, and then she told me that when her husband got out of the hospital that he weight one hundred and eleven pounds, and that he weight one hundred and fourty four and a half pounds and that he was doing real good, and now it is six months after his operation January the thirty first two thousand and three and it is his wifes birthday, and not only was it her birthday but also the day she would retirer from her factory job of thirty five years which was Senco in Mt. Carmel Ohio and her husband was so proud and thankful that he was still alive to see her accomplish all this, and all I could think was how this man was rebuilding his life for his wife and their children and was building a relationship with God, because you could just see how thankful this man was and how humble he had become and then his wife told me that when her husband would go to chemo. he would be setting their and if he would see anyone one standing their to get their treatment he would get up and give his seat to them and he would just stand their and smile, and when I herd this I knew that I was right when I said this man had become humbled, because here he is allready supposed to be dead, and he is more worried if someone else has a seat and is comfortable, other than him self and I would have to say that this act of kindness brought him unspeakable joy to his heart. Now this man had his whole colon removed and he never had a colostmey bag on his side and he had about six more weeks of cancer treatments left, and he, and his wife told me that the chemo. was not even making him sick, and I would have to say that his doctor was without anyway to explain this, because everyone I have ever talk to would allways tell me how sick they would feel after these type of treatments. Now his wife told me a little story about what her husband had done for them on Valentines Day and I would like to share this story with you. Her husband goes out and finds this cute little puppy that is ten weeks old and her and her husband named the little puppy Precious and you could feel the joy that this brought to this mans wife as she told the story to me, and then she went on to say, how well her husband was doing, and that her husband and her pastor was traveling to South Carolina on a missionary trip, and that her husband was telling people what God had done for him through all his sickness and how God lifted his spirit up so that he could work for the kingdom of God, and from South Carolina they would go to Kentucky to the pastors uncles Church were the pastors uncle was the pastor, his name was Charles Martin and when they returned the pastor would tell his church how much this mans testimonie touch their lives and how it would help others to walk in their faith, and the compassion that this man would show to others was unspeakable here he was telling people that he had never met, what God had done for him, and that he was being an example of Gods mercy, grace, love, patients, kindness, and that he willing lee done all of this with joy in his heart, and if the doctors would have been right this man would have been dead four months ago because now this man has been alive four seven months, and was traveling arround telling how thankful he was, when the doctor said to the family seven months ago just make him comfortable as you can, and the pastor said I never heard this man complain about any pain. So I would have to say, that it sounds like to me that Gods mercy made this man comfortable, and that Gods grace kept this man humble and alive for everyone to see, and that Gods love taught this man to love others, and that Gods patients taught this man, good things come to those who wait on it, and that Gods kindness taught this man to be kind to everyone all of the time, and you could just tell that he was willing to learn as much as he could from God.

Now this man had been talking to his youngest son about joining the chruch and his son, would just say, dad I believe in God but I feel that I don't need Church. Now this man never got mad, or discourage he would just say thats ok. Now the youngest son told me that he and his wife had got into some finacial debt and that it was three weeks before Christmas and they never had the money to buy their children any presents, because it was winter time, and he installed windows and hung viynal siding for a living and that their just was not a whole lot of this type of work at this time of the year. So the son told me that he was praying that God would send him some work. He told God that he would do whatever it took to get the work done, and that he just wanted his children to have a nice Christmas, and to have some presents to open. So he, and his wife prayed all that week just for the work, he was not asking God for the money, or for someone to give it to him, he wanted just enough work to buy his family some gifts for Christmas, and now he only had two weeks left, and he said that he knew something was about to happen, that he could just feel it. So when he went to work that Monday morning two weeks before Christmas his boss told him that he had for him sixty windows to install. Now this is alot of work and the type of windows they were, and the old house that they were in this job would not be easy, but this man's son now had a chance to earn the money before Christmas. He said that he knew that God had got him this work, because this was very unusall for this many windows, for that time of the year. So he thank God and told God how thankful he was and that he would get this done, and do whatever it took, and he knew that he only had two weeks to get all this work done. So he had his oldest daughters husband to help, they would start early in the morning and they wouldn't quit untill after dark, and he told me that either one of them wouldn't complain, and as hard as this job was, that this job was going smooth, and everyday on this job he would look to the sky and just say thanks. So the end of the second week came and the job was done, and the man's son had told his wife I know that God Blessed us with this money to buy Christmas for our children, and we are not even saved, or going to church and still God answered our prayers that we prayed. So the man's youngest son and his wife had one of the best Christmas they ever had and they were thankful to God, for he had blessed their family, in their time and need, and they knew it. Then the son told me how he went to pray to God for his wife, he told me that when he went to pray, he told God it's me again, but this one is not for me, it is for my wife, and that she wants to lose weight and she has been having a hard time, and I know that you answered my last prayer so would you please answer this one for her, and then he told me with in two months she had lost her weight that she wanted to lose. Now he and his wife was really fealing blessed and they both was very thankful and they really had a hard time explaining why God was doing the things that he was doing for them, but at the sametime they knew in their hearts that it was God and only God. Now he told me about one more prayer, he said, that God it's me again and I feal not worthy of what you have allready done for me, but I have one more prayer I have been doing siding and windows most of my life, and my family has to struggle every winter, and I don't want them to have to go through this any longer so would you help me to get another job. Then after this prayer he prayed, he was talking with a man that he had growed up with and went to school with, and this man asked him if he would come to work as a auto mechanic at his bussiness, and the only way that he had known how to do this type of work was that his grandfather had taught him and his brother how to work on cars. So he really didn't have to consider this, because he said, that he knew God was answering his prayer, and he accepted the job. Now he told me that God had answered three of his prayers, and if God would answer his prayers for him, and he was not even going to church. That he and his wife needed to go to church, so they began to go to the church where his father, and mother, and sisters went. Now his father had told me how proud he was of his youngest son, and that his youngest son was reading the bible, and studing, and learning Gods word, and was going to chuch every Sunday. You could just hear and feal this man's joy that he had, because of his son, and the man said, that he had allmost his whole family in his church, except his oldest son. He would ask his oldest son and the son would say that he believed in God, and that he didn't need church. So the man just told his oldest son that's ok, and that he loved him. Now it is seven months after this man's operation and the date is February the twenty first of two thousand and three, and the man's wife told me that her husband was very happy and excited he was leaving on a men's retreat with his youngest son. This would be his first time of doing anything like this with his son, but she also knew that it would not be the last, and she went on to say, that on February the twenty eighth of two thousand and three that her, and her husband, and their son an law, and their grand daughter was going to Las Vegas for a Nascar race which her, and her husband was very fond of, and they both loved Dale Earnhardt, and Dale Earnhart Jr.

Now when they got back from their trip her husband told me how good of a time they had, and that they were very tried, because it was 5:20 AM when they return to home, but he said, it was worth it, for they had such a great time with their son an law, and their grand daughter. Then his wife went on to tell me that her husband's chemo had to be strenthed, and that so far he was doing real good, but that this may make him sick, or lose his hair, and then she said, we just have to put it in God's hands and trust in him. Then I talked to her a few days later which was March the twentyth two thousand and three, and she said so far he has not been sick, and that he is still doing good, and all we can do is pray, because God has been so good to this family with all his blessings, and she said we praise God for it all, and then she told me that her husband, and their pastor was going on another trip on March the twenty fourth two thousand and three, to Lake Erie to pray with a woman who has cancer in her lungs. Now I have to say here this man was suppose to only have three months to live, and now it has been eight months and what is he doing, he is not laying around waiting to die, but he is going from place to place, and now he is going to pray with his pastor for someone else who has cancer my words cannot even begin to describe how much courage this man had to have, and the passion that he showed for others in their time and need, not even considering his self dieing with cancer. I would have say this is an example of true love for God, and Gods people.

This is now his nineth month, and the month is April two thosand and three his wife was telling how good this month has been to her husband. That he started the month off with gaining about three pounds, and that his weight was now up to one hundred and fourty eight pounds. Then she went on to tell me that her husband had went on another revival with their pastor to Clay County, Kentucky, and then she said that the Chemo was causing him to lose some of his hair, so he just shared his head, she also said that he didn't look bad, but that it looked good on him, and she told me what happen on Easter Sunday, that the young man that was their pastor's Armor Barrier asked her husband if he would take over for him, she said, that this made him feal so blessed, and that he was honor to be able to do this, plus everyone thought who could know the pator better, because these two men was together allmost everyday if not traveling to revival, or praying for someone, or on a retreat, then they would just fish, or golf, and then on April the thirty of two thousand and three, she said, that her husband was doing so good, and that his weight was now one hundred and fifty two pounds, and that the doctor was going to cut back on his dosage of chemo, and that he would only take that for four weeks and then she began to tell how her husband was setting up for a golf touramet, and that he was doing this to raise money for the mens group at church and that he couldn't wait to play in this tourment, and then I thought this man is an example for anyone who would have cancer, or any other sickness, or fatal disease, because I have been finding out what this man has been going through now for ten months, and now he is raising money for the mens group and, I would have to say that is putting others before his self, and he has showen everyone through Gods mercy, and grace never quit when the doctors tell you it is over, because everything this man has done, he done it through Gods mercy, and Gods grace and he never once blamed God he told me that he thank God that he was able to do what he was doing, and that it is never over untill God says it is done, and I would say that this man is living proof and that this started ten months ago from a hospital bed when he excepted Jesus into his heart, and excepted Jesus as his Lord and Saviour and then I believe God cleansed him with Jesus's blood and restored life into a body, that the doctor, said just make him comfortable he's not going to make it, and now I would have to say never quit just allow God to tell you when you are done and allways believe that Jesus is the only way to peace, and joy, and to heaven.

Now it is June two thousand and three and it has been eleven months that I have been writing about this man and his family and that I have witness how God has pulled this family through their crisis, almost losing their father, and if you talked to anyone of them they would tell you, all we can do is thank God. Then I was talking to this man and he began telling me about his fishing trips that him and his friends had been going on and how many fish they had caught, and that he was going to have a fish fry for their church, and charge five dollars a plate. Then he told me that he was doing this to raise the money to remodel their church, and that he would be the one to cook the fish and to serve the fish. Then I was talking to their pastor and he told me how great the fish fry went and that this man cooked every piece of fish and served it, and he also said the man was not feeling the best, but that he wanted to do this, and that he didn't want know help, and that the money they raised painted the inside of their church, and bought them a new drop ceiling, and built them an altar, and then he said, that the man was so proud of his youngest son because he done alot of the work and that he did a real nice job on everything he done, plus he built a roughed cross that they placed on the wall were the altar was. I'am just lost for words, because this man and his son just keep amazing me here they both are, and they are just on fire for God and Jesus doing everything that they possibly can, and doing it correctly for their church, and their Pastor, and if I had to say they both were doing it for God, and Jesus, and their family, and they were doing it willing lee, and with a joyful heart, and their is so much that we all can learn just from how these two men went about doing these type of things for their church, and how they was happy to be able just to do it, and never complaining, and you would never known that they done any of this, except that I talked to them about what they were doing, so that I could share it with you, and that I was impressed how God was working with them and their family and how this family was pulling it together for God and God's people. I would like to explain, and remind you it is now August two thousand and three and it has been over one year, and this man is still alive, and the doctor only gave him three hours at first and when he went past that the doctor gave him three days, and when he went past that the doctor gave him three months and said; just make him comfortable, and when the man went past that the doctor said; I cannot explain why he is still alive, but if their is anything that I learn it was that this man one year ago except Jesus Christ as his Saviour, and he claimed all this to be his own fault, he never blamed God, and I believe that he was reborn from that moment on, and remember he only ask God for one year, but I'am a witness he is still going strong, and he was telling me that he was going to Joplin Missouri in November two thousand three to a church called Camp Joy Ministries to give his testimoney, and he was real excited because most of the people from his church is going with him and his pastor on this Mission Trip, and all that came to my mind was he ask God one year ago to give him one year to get it right for God and I will say from every thing that I have witness this man did get it right, and I know that God has shown him mercy, and grace, and love, and God has blessed him with more than he even ask for, and I would say it came from this man keeping his word to God, and I also know that this man never complain about anything that he had to go through for this sickness, and he never complain about anything he done for his Church, and I would say that came from this man's love for Jesus because he knew that he would have died in that hospital if it would not have been for Jesus saving him on that day in two thousand, and two, and I would add that this man was showing more faith, then my words could explain, and I would say from everything this man has gone through, it was his faith in Jesus and God that kept him walking through this, and this man has set and example for all of us how your faith in Jesus and God can work for you and your family, and what I have learn by watching all of this is it starts with Jesus, and a step in faith and to trust God on your every circumstance, and allways ask God exactly what you want him to do, so you will know when God bless's you, and we must credit this man for his prayers and understanding of God's word and for him claiming everything he recieved from God by his faith, and his perseverance.

This is now the end of October two thousand and three and I had talked to this man's pastor he began to tell me that him and this man had been playing golf alot through the months of September, and October, and that they was really enjoying the time that they was get to spend together, and that their relationship was growing closer together for both of them if that was possible, because they were allways together and they were allready like father and son, and the pastor also said; that you would never know this man was sick he would just allways be thinking of others, and that he was hitting the golf ball better and further than he ever did before, and he had been talking to this man about his oldest son, and that the man thought that he was going to be hard to get him to turn his life around, but that he wouldn't give up, but that he would just pray and he would just trust in God and the pastor also said; this man knew if he could get his son in to the church he would be just like the younger son, and give it all he had, but this man would never force it on to his son he would just ask him, and when his son would tell him not right now the man would just say that's ok, and I love you know matter what you decide, but I believe the man knew it was just a matter of time and that his son would be there with him and the rest of his family, and you know this man never got mad, or discouraged he just kept a posetive attitude even when it came to his sickness, he just never gave up he would just keep on going like nothing was wrong and as I sat here writing this part to you I thought about what his pastor told me that this mans testimonie had touched alot of people and that the people and his own church just loved this man and I realized why, this man would allways think of others first and that he showed compassion for others even though he was so sick it was because he had the love of Jesus in his heart, and soul, and I believe when you have that on the inside that it has know choice but to show on the outside, and I knew at this moment that is what was happening, because everytime I saw this man he had a glow on his face, and this was a man that was not even suppose to be alive by what the doctors was saying for it has been sixteen months that he lived without a colon and never had a Colostomy bag, and the doctor said, he would be lucky to make it three months, and sixteen months later here he is golfing allmost everyday with his pastor,

I must say that a supernatural miracle has taken place in this mans bodie, because their is no other way to explain what has been going on for sixteen months except it is not over untill God says it is over and when we can turn to God, and not blame him for our sickness or what ever is going on with us that is when God will turn it around for us and our family, I do believe that, because this man is living proof, and no one could explain except God.

We are now in November two thousand and three and the man was doing good and he decide to renuie his wedding vows so he told his oldest son what he and his mother was going to do and envited him and his girlfriend, and the son said: as I was setting in church that day it was like he could see the truth about Jesus and how he need to go to church and that his dad was right and as the son told the father, a small tear fell to his cheak and father just smiled and said ok. So you can imagine the joy this man must have fealt now his whole family was going to church. But now when thanksgiving came the man became ill again so ill he couldn't even eat dinner. The family wanted him to go back to the hospital, but the man said: no, not untill you all eat your dinner. So you could imagen how fast that family ate that dinner, a then he allowed them to take him back to the hospital. Now when that next Sunday come the oldest son wanted to give his life to Christ, but he wanted to wait on his father to get out of the hospital, and as he and his girlfriend was setting their they had and altar call and girlfriend said: lets go now and they went. When the son got out of church he couldn't wait to get to the hospital and tell his father and his dad was very sick but you could see and feal his joy as the son told him what had happen, and when the next Sunday came which was December the six two thousand and three, the man got to go home not with his family but God had called him home and when he was laying their about to take his last breath his family and their pastor and the pastor's wife was praying that God would take him and the oldest son said he is gone.

I wrote this man's testimoine because I felt that God had called me to do it so it could help others who might me going through this samething, and you can see untill his last day he was still putting others first, and the reason I knew this man's life so well is I'am his oldest son and by the mercies of God and his Grace I was able to do this, because this was the hardest thing I have ever had to do, but Jesus gave me the strength, and this man's name is Philip Leo Royse Sr. and his wife is Barbra Ann Royse and their children are Philip Leo Royse II and his children are Dawn, Philip III, Tanna, and Chloe. James Kieth Royse and wife Tammy Royse and their children Tina, Kelly, James II, and Robert. Marcy Ann Buck and husband Jeff Buck and their children Holly, Jeffery II, Heather, and Isaac Jody Shabastian and husband Bobby Shabastain and their children Nick, Tyler, Halie, and Corie. Amy Felts and husband John Felts no children yet.

Now it is one year and six months after my father's death and the time is May two thousand and five and the next chapter's of my book is to reach out and help Reborn Christians and to encourage them as they walk in Faith by God's Grace Jesus's Love and the Holly Spirit to Guide you.

This chapter is in Rebrance of Philip Leo Royse Sr. who loved Jesus with his whole heart and done so much for his Church Harvest Rain Ministries and Loved Pastor Gordon Martin, and his family, and the whole conergation, and his new address is on the Golden Streets in Heaven. I want to give GOD thanks for my Father, and give GOD all the Honnor and Glory for his Grace towards my father and to let GOD know I understand now why he made my Father Lay Down To Look Up, and this was for you DAD.

Let's pray, Dear Heavenly Father we praise you for Your Son Jesus and we give Your thank's for this day, and we ask for guidance for the people that read this book that you would shead your grace upond their heart and that You would keep them strong so that they would never give up, or quit for the trials we must endure is to rebuild our faith in You, and we pray that we all sow the seed that you sent to pay that we all could be more like your Son Jesus Christ and walk in unity, meekness, and love, and have the patience we need to wait on Your will and purpose, we give You all the honor and glory in Jesus precious name.

Amen.

MERCY

Dear friend when we come to the Lord, we feal that we are not worthy, of the least of God's mercy, and the truth is we are not, because of sin, for God is holy, and pure, but when Jesus came for us, he boar our sins in his own body, on the cross, so that we could live unto righteousness, and by his stripes we are healed (refer. 1 Peter 2:24). And on that day, at Calavary when they crucified our Lord, was the ultimate example of God's mercy for us all who love's Christ Jesus, and I can only imagen God by his mercy standing, in front of the gate's of Heaven holding his Angels back from wanting to destroy the human race, but that is the kind of God we serve, he is merciful, he is faithful, and he promised to show mercy to the ones that love him (refer. Ex. 20:6), and when we are of Christ, we must allway's confess our sin's, and we must never try to hide, or cover up our sin's we must always repent (refer. Matt. 3:2), Repent means to have a change of mind and that will result into a change of conduct, Repentance will not arise within us, but God's mercy will lead us to repent, but we should never go, and sin willfully, (deliberately) after we have recieved the knowledge of the truth, we do that we are disobeying God, we are being unfaithful, & we have broken our agreement with God, what I mean is we cannot say we are going to go, and do something knowing it is wrong, and say well I just will repent. Now my friend we must know that we are not perfect, and we are going to make mistake's, but when we slip, and fall, God did give us Jesus to pick us back up, to make us stronger, and when we have truely excepted Christ, and we have the love of Christ in our heart, we will not deliberatly sin, we will try to sin less everyday, and we will know that God has forgiveness for those that love Christ, and didn't sin willfully, God will forgive us for our sins through the blood of Christ according to the riches of his grace (refer. Eph. 1:7), and sense God forgives us, we as Christians, should allways be forgiving in our attitude towards others, and never hold a grudge against anyone. (refer. James 5:9)

My friend release is alot like mercy, (release means to set free from confinement), and it is God's mercy that release's us from our sin's which confines us, it start's with God's love for us, which activates God's compassion for us, which activate's God's grace for us, which give's us God's mercy which gave us the cross, and the love of Christ our saviour. If we truely want God's mercy we must give mercy, and be merciful in every circumstance from the smallest, to the largest, it might just take a kind word, or a little patience. It might take some compassion, or us showing that we care. It might just take a little understanding, & it will take alot of our love. My friend when we see a family member, or a brother, or sister in Christ, or a coworker or a friend hurting, or in troubled time's, or what ever the promble might be, we want to give that person mercy. What we could do is put ourselves, in their skin, and begin to truely feal their hurt, and their pain, & when we put ourselve's in their position, we will feal their pain. That's when you will release your mercy. You will become merciful, and in return God will show mercy, and will give understanding, so that we can help in their prombles. But allway's remember to give thank's unto the Lord; for he is good; for his mercy endureth for ever (refer. 1 Chr. 16:34) and (refer. PS. 136:1)

Dear friend we as Christians know to pray for those who make us mad, and to never hold onto anger, that we can just release it at the feet of Jesus, but my friend we also need to realize where the anger is coming from, for their seem's to be so much in the world, at our home's, in our work place's, in public place's, on our highway's, just about every where ever you look, you can find someone that is mad, or angry. And we all know their are many things that can provoke anger. We know that jealousy is one that can provoke anger, and it brings envy, and strife, now jealousy mean's suspicious or fearful of being replaced by a rival; resentful or bitter in rivalry; demanding exclusive love, and envy mean's to have resentment for someone else's possessions, or advantage's, and strife mean's a bitter conflict between enimies; a fight or a struggle. Now what we want to do, if we ever own any of these feelings is to take them before the throne of Jesus, so that he can release us by his mercy so that we are not confined to these feelings, all our emotions does not run wild. If anyone has these fealings toward us we must know that we are to pray, and ask God why are they jealous, why are they angry, and then just start to thank God, and trust God, according to his will, and purpose, that he will deal with their heart, and that he will give understanding. We must pray that God will give them mercy, because I truely believe when we ask for God's mercy for other's, we are opening the door of mercy, and we are proving our love in Christ, that He lives within us, and we are proving that we hold no envy, or strife, towards them. The best thing we can do when the anger come's our way, is to be patient, careing, and loving, while we wait for God's will, and try to not give a mean response to anger, for we will just be adding fuel to the anger (refer. Prov. 15:1) Just try to find a sincere complement to give to that person, for when we came with, love it will never fail us, it will keep our peace, it will keep our joy, and it will keep our happiness in our heart. You see my friend, love is strong, and jealousy, and anger is cruel (refer. Song 8:6), and we must know that true love cannot be destroyed, for Jesus is love, and he is our strength. Only destruction will come to the ones that are workers of iniquity (refer. Prov. 10:29) iniquity is a grievous violation of justice; wickedness; sinfulness. But Christ want's us to show mercy to other's (refer. Luke 10:37), and he is the ultimate example of giving forgiveness, and mercy toward's other's. When Jesus was on the cross he cried out Father forgive them; for they know not what they do (refer. Luke 23:34).

Then their is also a lot of hurt, and anger that will come from someone's past. Where we make the mistake is to hold onto the pain of the past, when we should be going to the Lord, and releasing the past so that we can be free of the confinement of the pain, move onto the future, with a new way of living, which Jesus has allready made for us, (refer. Heb. 10:20). You see my friend, Christ is our new and living way, by which we can go to the holy place of God, but if we let our past poision our future, and if we do not let go of the old, God cannot give us new. The truth is God makes all things new, and his words are true, and faithful (refer. Rev. 21:5), for those who love his Son, and we as Christians should replace our sinful anger, with the righteousness of our Lord (refer. Eph. 4:31-32).

Dear friend let us pray together, Dear Heavenly Father we give thanks for the Son of God our Saviour, we give you thank's for your word, we thank you for your mercy, that we receive through the blood of Christ, and we ask that we maybe more merciful towards others, that we may give mercy freely in our everyday life, that mercy would remain in our heart, and that we all would never hold onto our anger, that we would just release it to our Lord, so that he can turn our anger, into love, and mercy, so that he can replace our harsh word's, into gentle, and kind word's, that we would not hold grudges, and that we could give an encouraging word, instead of a discouraging word, that we would come together, in unity, and be more caring for other's in everything we do, give us the strength to brake the barrier's of denomonation's so that we can all come together, and be the body of Christ for your honor, and your glory, and that your mercy would be with those who love your Son, and we ask it all in Jesus precious name, and we give you all the glory, Amen.

My friend when we have been born again by God's mercy, he is showing his true love for us, when we excepted Jesus as our Lord, and Saviour, God then gives us the Holy Spirit which will put mercy in our heart, which will make us more merciful in our attitudes, and our conduct, towards other's. Being merciful, is to be compassionate, and to treat others kind. For God is so merciful, so we should be merciful (refer. Luke 6:36). Now if we as Christians can get mercy deep into our heart, and our spirit, this will activate the compassion we need to give to other's, this will also produce the kindness we need to show to others, you see this is God's word, and we must humble ourselve's to it, and be obedient to the truth of the gospel of Christ, but always know to seek our redemption in God's mercy, never think that it is to come from our works, for it will only come from our faith, in Christ, never think that we could obtain God's mercy by religious achievement, we must go boldly to the throne of grace, that we may obtain mercy, and find grace to help in our time of need (refer. Heb. 5:16), only Christians posses such boldness, and it is only possible because of Christ, the throne is a place of authority, it is the only place a christian can go to obtain God's mercy, and grace in our time, and needs, and it is thank's to Jesus, for he fought the battle of sin and He obtain God's mercy for us all who love Him, and He gave us the victory over sin for his body asorbed the sin of this world, and I can only imagen the pain of sin of this world, our Lord had to endure when he hung on the cross, when God's wrath was poured upon His own Son for our sin's, who was accursed of God as our sin-bearer. Now we must realize as a Christian to love our Lord, our king, our Saviour, more than anyone, or anything, for He loved us first, and He is the author of love that abides in you and I, and when He is loved backed, He will produce compassion, and kindness in our heart, that will allow us to reach out to the sick, those inprision, the homeless, those who are hungry, those who are thirsty, those who need our love, those who are lost, Jesus say's we are Blessed for being merciful (refer. Matt 5:7), Mercy in this verse is a reference to us that was born again by the mercies of God, so is it not, our reasonable service to God to be merciful to all people. For no eye has seen, no ear has heard, no mind has conceived, what God has for those who love Him (refer. 1 Cor. 2:9).

Dear friend we all know that God judges our heart, and we know that their are many diffuclt circumstance's that come into our lives almost everyday, and we must know that we as Christians, are not to run from trouble, but to stand firm in God's word, and His will, and allways pray for every circumstance, to allow God to work out our promblems, this shows total trust in God, because if we do not, and we just hold on to trouble in our heart, we are sinning (refer PS. 66:18), and we all must know that something is going to bring trouble to our heart, but we can not hold on to that trouble, if we do we are focusing on the trouble, when we should be focusing on the Lord, we are telling God that we do not trust Him to get us through the trouble, we are telling God that He does not see, or hear our trouble, but when you can go to the Lord, and release trouble's, this is when we prove our trust in the Lord, and that we will not be confine to our troubles, and in the moment of trouble we need to find the strength to worship God, and thats when we will find God's mercy, and He will hear our prayer's (refer. John 9:31).

My Friend when we dedicate ourselves to the word of God, we are surrendering to the will of God which is His desire, and wish for His people. That those who believe in His Son will have enternal life, and that none of His people would be lost (refer John 6:39-40), and when our live's revolve around the word of God we are opening the door for God's mercy, which He will bring His righteousness into us, for our lives, and by that we become a living sacarfice (refer Rom 12:1), and in Romans Paul encourages, and urges the Christians at Rome to allow God to transform their minds to know the perfect will of God (refer. Rom. 12:2), that is, we as Christians must allways seek God's word to find the true will of God, and fully committ to doing the will of God, as He reveal's His will through the word of God, and by our obedience to God, will bring His mercy, with His blessing into our home's. Jesus taught his disciples to pray for God's will to be done on earth as it is in Heaven (refer. Matt. 6:10), and we should take this as an example of what Jesus want's us all who believe's in Him to do, just pray for God's will to be done on earth, as it is done in Heaven. You see my friend we need to pray for the future city which is New Jerusalem that God built as a dwelling place for those who belong to Him (refer. Heb. 11:10-16), or Paradise which describes the heavenly home of the redeemed (refer. 2 Cor. 12:4), this is a place worth praying for, where God dwells eternally amoung the redeemed (refer. Rev. 21:2-10) We are the redeemed, and where ever God has planted us in the Body of Christ we are to grow from thier, we are to come together as one accord (purpose or mind) in prayer and supplication (every occasion or circumstance) and work together for the vision that God gave the leader or Pastor of our Church (refer. Acts 1:14), and so that we can be succesfull we need to do it with joy, in our heart, do all things without murmurings (complaining) and disputings (arguments) (refer. Phil. 2:14), and when we all pull together we are the Body of Christ. Paul identified the Church as Christ's Body (refer. Col. 1:24), Paul tell's us that the risen Christ dwell's in his body, and persides of the Church (people) (refer Eph. 1:19-23), Paul tell's us Christ assigns spiritual gifts to His Body to accomplish His work and to bring us as believers to maturity (refer. Eph. 4:7-13)

Paul also tell's us that member's of the body are to care for one another, and if one member suffer, all the members suffer with it or one member be honored, all the members rejoice with it. Now we are the body of Christ (refer. 1 Cor. 12:25-27), and since we are Christ's Body, our actions and attitudes toward one another should allways reflect His character. Now we would have to say; when we can pull together and become one accord this is what the Lord say's Church is all 'about, a local body of believers assembled for Christian worship (refer. Acts 15:4), as well as all the redeemed of the ages who belong to Christ (refer Gal. 1:13), and when we Belong to Christ, Christ lives with in us, and the life we now live, we must live by faith of the Son of God, who love's us, and gave Himself for us (refer Gal. 2:20) My friend the truth is, the nature of the flesh will complain, will be arguementive, but that is not of the Spirit of God. When we are of Christ, and we see or hear anything that we think is wrong, in our family, or our Body of Christ, or were ever the promblem may lie, we are not to down people, for what they are doing, or saying, because we are not the judge, but what God want's us to do, is to go to prayer ask God for His mercy for them, for this is a spiritual warfare, and without prayer and God's armor it is impossible to get the victory, that is when Satan attacks with confussion, and anger. We are not just to pray for ourselves, but for all God's people, for spiritual combat is both an individual, and corporate matter. So please when we see something wrong do not complain to another, but trust God and pray for their faith (refer Eph. 6:18) for these are not my words, but they are God's for those who genuine love Jesus as our king, our Lord, our Saviour, for He was sent to save the world, not to condemn (refer. John 3:17), and sense Jesus choose to go through with God's plan, for His love for us. Then shouldn't we want to love Jesus more than anyone, shouldn't we want to know the word of God, shouldn't we want to walk in faith, shouldn't we want to walk in truth, shouldn't we want to love each other, shouldn't we want to love our parent's, shouldn't we want to love our brother's, and sisters, shouldn't we want to cherish our wives, shouldn't the wife's want to help their husbands, should we want to love our children, shouldn't we want to to visit the one's in prison, shouldn't we want to pray for others, shouldn't we want to trust God for good, and bad, shouldn't we show compassion for the homeless, shouldn't we want to buy a child shoe's for their feet or clothe the one's that need our help, shouldn't we want to feed the needy, shouldn't we want to pray for the sick, shouldn't we want to share the gospel, shouldn't we want to be patient on God's will, shouldn't we want to fellowship with Christians, shouldn't we want to encourage other's, shouldn't we want to be a blessing to other's, shouldn't we want to be obedient to God, shouldn't we want to starve the flesh, shouldn't we want to feed the spirit, shouldn't we want to pray for our enimies, shouldn't we want to dispise anger, shouldn't we want to hate all evil, shouldn't we want to rebuke Satan. My friend if you simply said; yes, then you are being mercieful, and praise God for He is worthy of all the

Glory, and when we say yes, we will want to do what Jesus told us; He that believeth on me, the work's that I do shall he do also; and greater works than these shall he do; because I go unto my Father. And whatsoever you shall ask in my name, that will I do, that the Father may be glorified in the Son, (refer. John 14:12-13) This is Jesus's promise for us, to have unlimited resource's to do the works of God.

When we truely except the love that Christ has for us, this is when we will experience loving kindness, which is God's gentle, and steadfast love, and mercy which He extends freely to His people (refer. Ps. 103:4-12), these are spiritual blessings, which reflect's God's character, and His greatness of His mercy, which is His compassion for us, and God's mercies are abundant (refer. 1 Pet. 1:3), by the resurrection of Jesus from the dead God is reconciled with us, which saved us from the world, and brought us into the presence of God which give's us new life, that will begin at salvation. My friend it is God's mercies that we are not consumed, because His compassion will not fail us. His mercies are new every moring, great is his faithfulness (refer. Lam. 3:22-23) God's faithfulness is permanent, is secure, is reliable, and when we believe; that is genuine faith in God's mercies. Jesus show's us by example to have compassion for other's, when he showed compassion for the multitude (refer. Matt. 15:32), but what we need to understand, we are the multitude, and the Lord expect's His follows to show compassion toward other's (refer. Matt. 18:33), and when we are saved we are forgiven by God's mercy, but we are also to be merciful, and forgiving, because unforgiving people prove that they have never been born of God. But one thing we must allway's remeber, is that, if someone has not reached Salvation yet, God can change someone by His mercy, or according to His will and purpose, so if we ever see, or hear of this fruit being bared, please try not to be quick to judge, but we can be quick to pray for that person, for we don't know God's plan. Dear friend, it allway's helps if we look back and remeber, before we was given the gift of Salvation, we to bared bad fruit, and we was walking in darkness, and it was God's mercy that brought us to the light. When Paul wrote to the Ephesians, he told them, for you were once darkness; but now are you light in the Lord: walk as children of light (refer. Eph. 5:8) Paul is reminding them were they use to be, but at the same time he encourage's them to focus on the Lord. I believe when we remeber were we came from, and can confess that we were wrong, we can help people that are still their, and we can become the Paul of today, and encourage other's, by just being an example of goodness, and righteousness, and truth. (For the fruit of the Spirits in all goodness and righteousness and truth;) (refer. Eph. 5:9). It is God's will for us to confess our fault's to one another, for admitting, our wrongs will bring God's mercy, and God's will is to pray for one another, this will release God's compassion for the one who is prayed for, and for the one who is praying (refer. James 5:16) it is Gods mercy, and compassion for us, that brings us to pray for others, this is one reason we allways want to be thankful to the Lord, dear freind we must allways know that one prayers are too be of total trust in God, for He is so faithful.

In the Old Testament one of God's name was Yahweh-Rapha which in Hebrew spelling Yahweh meant Lord, Yahweh-Rapha meant The Lord That Heals You. Now we as Christians of today could be preventing some of the sickness's, that are caused by stress, worring, and even anger, by trusting our God as Yahweh-Rapha, and by allowing Him to deal with the promble's that bring trouble, and sickness, and when we totally trust God, and totally love His Son, we will find that God has hidden His commandment's in our heart, and we need to apply them to our life's, and for the Bible it is just a book, and alot of people have them in their Homes as decerations, and that is all it will be, unless we study it, and pray that God would reveal the scriptures, and once we begin to understand God's word, and apply it to our life's, then it become's more than a book, it become away of life, it become's Basic Instructions Before Leaving Earth, but we must try to be patient, for this will not all take place over night, it will take time to learn, and it will take time to apply it to your life, so please be patient, and to know that it help's when we surround ourselve's with loving Christian's to encourage us to stand strong in faith, to help us when we make a mistake, but if we don't have Christians to turn to, we do have God, and He will never fail us, for He sent His Son Jesus to love us, to encourage us, to strength us, to teach us to care for one, and another, and by His mercy, to love one, and another, and He showed us it is not love unless you give it away, for if we are not of love, we don't know God, for God is love (refer. 1 John 4:8).

Now dear freind when we all first come to the Lord we all need to realize that we, and Jesus are not compatable, and that Jesus will never change, and we will not either, unless we truely give our heart, and our life to his will, and then He will live with in us (refer. Gal. 2:20) and our change's will come with time, and patience's to wait on the Lord, and then we need to learn to lay our burden's at the feet of Jesus, this could be worry, doubt, anger, financial, sickness, this could be a number of thing's, but when we take it to the Lord, we must trust His mercy for us, and His love for us, and to show Him that we trust Him, we should never go back to the burden we left with Him, we are to wait on His will, and purpose, for God knows our needs and His plan, and He will sustain us, He will never permit the righteous to be moved (refer. Ps. 55:22) and as time goes along we should alway's remeber, when we excepted the love of Christ, and we gave our life to Him, and we confessed He is Lord, and we believed it in our heart that God had raised Him from the dead three days later we are saved, for it is with the heart we believe into righteousness, and with the mouth confession is made into salvation (refer. Rom. 10:9-10), and this my friend make's us the righteous, and we must show God we trust Him totaly, by seeking God first on every circumstane of our life this will prove our priority is spiritual, and then out of His mercy, will come his righteousness, and it is good to know where ever God would lead us, He will provide for our need's (refer. Matt. 6:33). So we as christians should never worry about tomorrow, for sufficeint unto the day is the trouble there of (refer. Matt. 6:34) we know each day will have it's own trouble's and challenges, but as christians our job is to handle them with responsiblty, and without worring about the promblems that could come tomorrow. The Lord knows that our worring will only bring sorrow and sickness, and that it will take our eye off of Him, this is why He told us to seek God first, for when we pray it is not only to ask, but it is also to recieve answers from God, it is to confess it is to be thankful, it is to fellowship with God, it is by our prayers we can seek, and talk with God, and we should start our prayers with our Heavenly Father, and give thanksgiving, and confessing our sin's, praying for our needs, and the needs of other's, and always end our prayer in Jesus's name, and we allway's want to humble ourselve's, and never be of selvish pride, for Jesus say's he that humbleth himself shall be exalted (refer. Luke 18:14) God hear's the prayer's of the humble, God answer's prayer's when we obey Him (refer. 1 John 3:22), when we confess our sin's (PS. 66:18), when we abide in Christ (refer. John 15:7), when we ask God according to His will (refer. 1 John 5:14) when we ask

God in faith (refer. Mark 11:22-24) when we allways have pure motives (refer. James 4:3), when we live peaceably with our wife's or husband's (refer. 1 Peter 3:7) now these are the Lords words, and we all must realize, and know if we are having diffucltings in one of the area's, or more this is when God's mercy comes to us, for this is why He planted us in the Body of Christ, so that we would have someone to turn to, so that we could encourage each other, so that we could pray for one, and another, so when we fall, we would have some ware to land, and to stand firm, and we must realize we are not perfect, but we must know that God is perfect, this is why we need to seek Him, in every thing that we do, seek is to look, seek is to hope, it is to look for what God has for us, and to hope by our faith, that we can make us about Him in everything we do. Dear friend, I have seen prayer's answered when people come together, and pray in one mind and one accord, for their is strength and power when we come together, so let's believe together, and pray. Dear Heavenly Father we give you thanks, and all the glory and we praise you, for the mercy, and the love that Christ has for us all, and we pray to be more like Christ, to have the strength to carry the cross, to love other's, to be more merciful, to be more caring, to be more humble, to be slow to speak, to be quick to hear, and we pray that You would give us understanding, that You would reveal Your word, according to Your will, and Your purpose, so that You would have the Glory in Your Son, and we pray if there be any sick amoung us, that we could go to the Throne of Jesus and that He would take us to Yahweh-Rapha the Lord of healing, and that we would trust Him to deal with the prombles that come with worring, anger, and just any sickness that we may have, and that we all come together to know the healing power of our All Mighty Living God the Father of Jesus our Saviour the Soul Creator the only Jehovah-Jireh that will provide for His people who believe in Him and His Son, and we humble ourselve's to thank you the God of Jacob for bringing us from the darkness, and making us, Your children of light, for You are the God of the people, and we worship only you for your marvelous works, and we pray that we never take them for granted any longer, and that we would reconize Your presence, and Your Hand over every circumstance in our live's, in our childrens live's, that our church would start at home, and that our candlestick would burn forever, and be the light that you choose for us, that You would continue to use us for Your Glory, and we pray for the Heavenly City the New Jerusalem that we would be the one's that You would dwell with forever, we pray to Our Father which art in Heaven, Hallowed be thy name, thy Kingdom come. Thy will be done in earth, as it is in Heaven. Give us this day our daily bread. And forgive us our debts, as we forgive our debtors. And lead us not into temptation, but deliver us from evil; for thine is the Kingdom, and the power and the glory, and every creature which is in heaven, and on the earth and under the earth, and such as are in the sea, and all that are in them, heard I saying Blessing, and honor and glory, and power be unto him that sitteth upon the throne, and unto the Lamb, for of Him and through Him, and to Him, are all things to whom be glory for ever, and ever, we thank thee, in Jesus's Holy name. Amen.

Dear friend alot of time's when we must go through some trials and test's, come's from God's mercy, because He love's us so much, most of the time God is remolding our character to be closer to His charcter, for we are made in His image (refer. Gen. 1:26) when God begins to work on our charcter we must be faithful, and allway's try to remember we are the servants, by being faithful, is to stand firm on what God's word say's, tring to never bend His word, for our comfort, and when we are servant's of God we must allway's be trusted and truthful in all we do, and if we are going to be trusted, and truthful, we must seek God first we must be totally honest with Him, we seek God so that He will guide, and teach us what He would have us to do, but please allways remember to listen, and ask God to confirm, what you ask, and allways be patient, for God is faithful, and He will confirm if it is of Him, and we can learned by God's mercy when we surrender to His will and His purpose, and He brake's us over the corner stone (which is Jesus), it is not only to remold our charcter to the image of God, it is also to deliver us from the temptations of the world (refer. 2 Peter 2:9), it is Gods mercy that surrounds us, with His Angle's, to protect, us from the world, and the temptation that are with in, for those who love His Son, and my friend it is when we can put our life to the side, or lay it down, for God and let Him start us over with His word, and fast, and pray, and apply His word to our everyday life, and allways trust God, and obey Him for what He wants, and this will begin to change our life's forever, and this will also have a domino effect in our families life, and our friends life, just by being an example of the changes Christ brought to our life, and this is when we will want to be a better Husband or Wife this is when we will want to be a better Father, this is when we will want to be a better Mother, this is when we will want to be a better son, or daughter, this is when we will want to be a better brother, or sister, this is when we will want to be a better friend, this is when we will want to love everyone, as our self, this is when we will want to be more humble, this is when we will want to be more forgiving, this is when we will want to be more merciful, this is when we will want to be more caring, this is when we will want to be more kinder, this is when we will want to be a better person, to have our charcter more like His, but this will only happen through trials, tests, and Gods love, and mercy for us, and our willingness to surrender our life's to the Father, the Son, and the Holy Spirit, so please be patient through the trials, and just walk through the door's as God open's them, and stand strong in your faith, and please allways remember we are winner's in the Body of Christ as long as we never give up, or quit, and hold tight to that taught because their are going to be time's, as a reborn christian you will want to hear, you are a winner, and as long as you never quit, God will make your enemies side with you, and God will give you the victory and He will exalt you before your pears. For, Thine, O Lord is the greatness, and the power, and the glory, and the victory, and the majesty: for all that is in the heaven, and in the earth is thine; thine is the Kingdom, O Lord, and thou art exalted as head above all. Both riches and honor come of thee, and thou reignest over all; and in thine hand is power and might; and in thine hand it is to make great, and to give strength unto all. Now therefore, our God, we thank thee, and praise thy glorious name (refer. 1 Chr. 29:11-13).

Now I would like to end this paragraph with a simple question that we all should ask ourselve's. What is good in my life today? I would have to be honest, if I would have asked myself this question two years ago I would not have much to say, but today is a differnt story, because God gave me His mercy, so now I can be quick to say; the Father, the Son, the Holy Spirit, my wife, my children, my Father, my Mother, my Brother, my Sisters, and their children, my Aunt's, my Uncle's, and their children, my friends, and their children, and last, but by know mean's least my new Family the Body of Christ, which I truely believe that God hand picked, and I'am so thankful, not just for the blessings, but for His love, that He choose me, before I ever consider Him, and this is why I want to lay my life down for Him, so I can make it all about Him, according to His will and purpose, and for the rest of my day's, I will pray for the strength to praise, and worship the only God the Father of Jesus the Lord of Lords, the King of King's, our Saviour, and I will cherish His word, and try to apply it to my life, for the Bible is,

B asic
I nstructions
B efore
L eaving
E arth

and now by God's mercy, I truely want to make my life about them,

T o   than I ever done before,
H elp
E ven
M ore

and I give the Lord all the honor, and glory forever, and ever, in Jesus Holy Name. Amen.

When we have come to our salvation, and we truely believe that Jesus is the Son of God, and He died for our sin's, and then God raised Him from the dead three day's later, we are truely saved (refer. Rom. 10:9-10), but let's go one step further, and ask ourselve's what do we have to do to have a relationship, or to fellowship with God? One of the first things we can do is seek God through our prayer's on every circumstance, but what we want to realize, is how important it is to listen to what God has to say through the Holy Spirit, and we as reborn christians also want to focus on obedience to fellowship with the Farther, the

Son, and the Holly Spirit for this will only come from us obeying God's voice, and keeping His commandments in our heart, and our every day life (refer. Jer. 7:23), you see my friend when we obey God's word we are building our own relationship with Him, and we are proving our love for our Saviour Jesus Christ, and we are walking with the Lord, and we must remind ourselves even though we are saved, and covered by the blood of the lamb, that God did give us freewill, and we still must make good choice's, from bad choice's, for God is not a controlling God, many time's we all have heard, if God did not want me doing this I would not be doing this, or if God did not want me to have this I would not have this, the truth is God want's us to just make good choice's based on the word of God, this is why it so important to study our bibles, and to ask elders questions when we do not unstand, or we can just go straight to the Lord, in our prayer's and seek His wisdom, for His wisdom is pure, and peaceable, gentle, and willing to yield, full of mercy and good fruits, without partiality, and without hypocrisy (refer. James 3:17). You see my friend if any of us lack in wisdom the bible say's; let them ask it of God, that giveth to all men liberally, and without reproach; and it shall be given, but we must allways ask in faith, with no doubts (refer. James 1:5-6), you see as we enter into our trials if we ask God for the wisdom He will show us the reason for our trials, or He could give us the wisdom to endure them, but it will only be given if you ask, and believe in your faith, seek, and you shall find; knock, and it shall be opened unto you. For every one that asketh recieveth; and he that seeketh findeth; and to him that knocketh it shall be opened (refer Matt. 7:7-8). This is the importance of prayer and a way for us to fellowship with God, by the nature of prayer is to just talk with God, and it will lead us to a successful Christian life, for God is not only concerned, about our Sunday's, for He is concerned about our Monday's, for He is concerned about our Tuesday's, for He is concerned about our Wedensday's, for He is concerned about our Thursdays, for He is concerned about our Friday's, for He is concerned about our Saturday's too, and we need to reconize His presence with us at work, at home, were ever we may go, because when we reconize God in our everyday life, and be thankful of His presence with us were ever we maybe, I would have to say that is more than just being saved, that is truely fellowshiping with the Lord, because we reconize He is with us were ever we go even though He would be their wether we would reconize His presence, or not, for that is the kind of God He is, and that is the mercy that He give's us all who truely love His Son Jesus. So now then if we are truely building a relationship with God, should we be concerned about our children, should we be concerned about family members, should we be concerned about the homeless or the hungry, should we be concerned with doing our job correctly, and on time, should we be concerned to love everyone, should we be concerned to pray everyday for every circumstance, should we be concerned to starve the flesh, should we be concerned to feed the spirit, should we be concerned with the evil of the world, should we be concerned to give and be thankful, should we be concerned for the trials we are to endure, should we be concerned to obey the word of God. Yes, and believe me if you are truely walking with the Lord you will have even more concerns, you see our concerns will become away of life, they will become our goal's, and we must realize if we did not have these concerns we would not love Christ, we would not be fellowshiping with the Lord, because we cannot worship God without accepting and loving Christ Jesus. For you see my friend if you love the parent, you will not hate the Son, you will know that the Father sent Him (refer. John 8:42), and Jesus told us if a man keeps my word he shall never see death (refer. John 8:51), and this is His promise, that we as christians can build our faith on for He is truth and love, and whatsoever we ask, we recieve of Him, because we keep his commandments, and do those things that are pleasing in his sight (refer. 1 John 3:22). My friend please allways remeber, that one of our best results of a life lived in purity before God is having a life where there is effective prayer. For right living will be an important part of succesful praying, and true faith in Christ will produce geniue love for others, for God is love, and every one that love's is born of God (refer. 1 John 4:7), now we must know that it was Gods love for us, that produce His mercy for us, to allow Christ to be crucified for our sins, and left alone to die for the sins of the world.

What I would like to say next, I want to put in story form, I would like us to picture this in our mind's as this being us before we were saved. Their stood a filthy man with dirty, and torn clothe's, and their stood God at the gate's of heaven looking down at this poor man, and by His mercy He turned to one of His Angel's and He said: I want you to go and get that man so he may be one of my son's, and the Angel went, but when the Angel got to the man, Satan jumped between them and said: he is mine, and then the Angel said: God wants this man as His son and what would be the price He would have to pay for this man, and the Satan said: it is law someone must die, and his blood must be spilled out. So the Angel went back to God, and told Him what Satan had said, and then God by His mercy look down at the man and said: tell Satan I will send my Son to die and spill his blood for this man, and many other men, that my Son will die to cover all sin, and Satan agreed, because Satan tought he was killing God's only Son, but he did not know it was God's plan to allow His Son to die for sin so that God would have many Son's, which is you, and I, because it was not the nails that held Him to the cross, it was His love for you, and I, and for God to give His only Son for a filthy little man is proof enough for me of His love that produced His mercy for us, and now God looks down on us and through the blood of Christ He see's us holy and pure, and every Christian can conquer sin, because Christ lives in him (refer. Gal. 2:20), and christian's must accept Christ and allow Him to live His divine life in them, so other's will see His influence and glorify God, you see this is what the Lord wants for us all, to let your light so shine before men, that they may see your good works, and glorify your Father which is in heaven (refer. Matt. 5:16), for these are the Lord's word's, and we all know that darkness cannot hide the light, that the smallest light can shine in the greatest darkness, and by excepting Jesus we are light, and the way we are going to shine, is to be example's to the world, of the love we have recieved from Christ from God's mercy for us all, and to be example's of that love is to love, is to care, is to be kind, is to encourage, is to feed the needy, is to clothe the naked, is to help the poor, is to spread the gospel, is to be humble, is to be slow to speak, is to be merciful, is to pray for your enemies, it is to serve other's, it is to be more like Christ, for there will be a day when we will all want God's mercy, and his question to will be what did you do for me? But, we all know if we have done these things for Jesus we will hear well done, thou good and faithful servant: thou hast been faithful over a few things, I will make thee ruler over many things: enter thou into the joy of thy Lord (refer. Matt. 25:21), and when you are a christian, and save by the blood of the Lamb, you wait your whole life to hear two word's "well done".

Now may I please take a moment to say from my heart how I truely feel about how God gave my Father his mercy, as you all know when my Father laid in that Hospital bed, and the Doctor said: he has three hours left, we had no ideal that God was going to touch my Father by His mercy, and as I look back my Father really never served God for fifty eight years, I know he believed in God he just never worshiped him, but now by God's mercy I know my father had a divine appoitment with Jesus, and I believe it was that day when the Doctor said, he has only three hours, but what the Doctor didn't know was my Father had a divine appointment with Jesus, because when my Father walked out of that hospital about two weeks later that Doctor told me he could not explain his fast recoverey, but now I know it was a simple word called mercy, and God gave my Father the best seventeen month's of his life to serve, and to worship Him, and my Father's divine appointment would come to touch my life because he lead me to the Lord for my divine appointment, and even though I never got to serve the Lord with my Father, because I was saved on a Sunday after Thanksgiving and the next Sunday my Father went to be with the Lord, but as I write this to you my friend I remember that Sunday our Pastor had prayed a prayer over me that I would take my Father's place in the Church, and now by God's mercy I believe I have, because my Father was our Pastor's Armor Bear and now I'am, my Father use to enjoy going on retreats with Pastor, and now I do, but God took it one step further, because in September of two thousand and six, God made it possible for me, and my wife to purchase my Father's House, from my mother, and I also bought the last vechicle he bought new and now I did not only take his place in the church, but God gave me his life I have his last car, I have his Home, I have his garage, I have all his tool's, and I have his job in the church, all because God showed my father His mercy, and I now go to church on Sunday with my wife my children, my mother, my brother, my sisters, and their children, and my aunt's, and my cousins, and we all serve God by his mercy, under the leadership of the Church Pastor Gordon, which who was my Father's best friend, and who he loved, and allway's said: that little red headed man has a direct line to God, and I truely thank God for making us all one big family, and I look forward to serving God in my Father's place with Pastor Gordon.

Now my friend allway's try to be merciful in all you do, and allway's remember if we never give up, or quit we have not failed, and always love because love will never fail you. So please try your best to love everyone, and I want to be thankful to God for Christ, and you my dear friend. By God's mercy may I share some truth with you. As we walk by faith with God's mercy, He will show us some things about ourselves that we might not like, or even want to believe, but God is of love mercy, and truth, so first He shows us how much He love us He give's us His only Son, second He show's us we was born of sin, and then by His mercy He show's us He has a plan, that He can cover us with the blood of His Son, and we can be born again, third He gives us His word which is full of His truth. You see my friend everything that I have shared with you so far I have been through, either by tribulation or just by fellowshiping with the Lord, and to be honest alot of things that He showed me about me I didn't like, and either did God, yet He loved me enough to have patients to walk me through step by step, and as He showed me by His mercy the things that I could change if I wanted, and then when I choose to change He gave me the love, and the knoledge, and the strength I needed, because through Him all things are possible, if we choose to believe. Dear friend even if we are saved we are still going to have to make choices from right to wrong, but what I have found out when I seek God first He give's me the right direction to take, He give's me the right choices to make, and He turn's my tribulation into something I can share with you, and I just want to encourage you my friend to stand strong in your faith, and stead fast in your prayer's, and try to always seek God first so that He can give you something to share, and we all should allway's be thankful, and give Him all the glory for He is worthy for those who believe, may God's mercy be with you and your family forever, and ever my friend. Amen.

GRACE

Grace was before the foundation of the earth. God wrote our names in the Lamb's Book of Life. His grace is a gift it is God's unmerited favor, and love towards us for our salvation (refer. Eph. 2:8). This is when we get to heaven, no one can say it was because of what I have said or done simply it is God's gift (refer. Eph. 2:9). For the law was given to Moses, but grace and truth came by Jesus Christ (refer John 1:17). It was God's grace that gave us the cross so that Jesus could redeem us from the curse of the laws (refer. Gal. 3:13). This leads God to grant salvation to believers through the exercise of their faith in Christ Jesus (refer. Titus 2:11). Salvation that appears to all of us is based on God's grace that provides salvation through the unlimited atonement of Christ and our faith within as believers. Salvation means "deliverance," and when God raised Jesus from the dead that gave us living hope. That we could now be delivered from our sins, by the Son of God, but only if we believe. Now if we believe there is an inheritance that no one can take away it will not fade away. It is reserved for us in heaven. This inheritance is kept by the power of God through faith into salvation. Here we are looking at final salvation. That is, deliverance from the presence of sin and into the presence of God. Now there are trials that we will endure. Try to remember they are only temporary. True faith can not be destroyed. Please keep in mind that God is in the process of rebuilding our faith through our trials. He will strengthen our faith, to know that He will get us through anything if we believe and trust Him (refer. 1 Peter 1:3-9). Now, the things of salvation are hope, holiness, Godly fear, and love. After we have come to the Lord, we want to try our best to focus on the things of salvation. Which is the hope of Jesus being the redeemer. The word redeem means "to purchase". That is when Jesus died for our sins. He paid the ultimate price that satisfied the demand of His Father's Holiness. The price of redemption was the blood of Jesus Christ (refer. 1 Peter 1:18-19). Which is revealed to us that believe in God. That God raised Christ from the dead, and gave Him glory; that our faith and hope might be in God (refer. 1 Peter 1:21). Keeping in our minds that we will come into thy house in the multitude of thy mercy: and in thy fear will we worship toward the temple of thy holiness (refer. Psalm 5:7) The fear of the Lord is clean, enduring for ever: the judgements of the Lord are true and righteous altogether (refer. Psalms 19:9) Seeing that we have purified our souls in obeying the truth through the Spirit that Jesus is the Lord, and that God raised Him from the dead. Be sincere and have love towards one and another with a pure heart. We are born again from God's grace. We are regenrated by the Holy Spirit through the word of God. Which communicates His offer of salvation to us. It will live and abide in us forever. This is the word which by the gospel is preached into us (refer. 1 Peter 1:22-25).

God's grace in its fullness was on a day, at Calavary when Jesus was hung on a cross to die for our sins, to bare our sins in His own body so that we could be dead to sin, so that we could live into righteousness and so that we would be healed by His stripe's (refer. 1 Peter 2:24). We can see here Jesus took our punishment. Imagen someone doing something really wrong and then blaming you wanting to punish you for it. How would this make you feal? I know how I would feel. First I would feel hurt then I would feel attacked for no reason. Then I would be angry, because I would know that I did nothing wrong. Then we begin to think how can I get even. This is what has been handed down through society from generation to generation its ok to get even. But Jesus tells us different. You have heard that it has been said. An eye for and eye, and a tooth for a tooth, But Jesus said: I say unto you, that you resist an evil person, and who ever shall slap you on your right cheek then turn the other to him also (refer Matt. 5:38, 39). What He is telling us is just because someone else has choosen to be an evil person, doesn't mean that we have to be, it is our choice to choose good from bad. Now imagne the God that rules the heavens and the earth from His throne and He decides to become a man, to come to the earth, and takes the blame for the sins that we have committed, so that we could have a chance to live in paradise with Him forever. And God never done no wrong, yet we blamed Him, we beat Him, we spit on Him, and then we crucified Him (refer. Mark 15:12-20). Instead of wanting to get even. He stood in front of us all, and fealt the pain of the sin of the world that has been passed down, from generation to generation. I feal ashamed, and I feal that God knew that He had to do this to prove to us that His love for us, is real, and that His love gave us His grace, which is His gift to everyone that believes in His Son Jesus Christ our Saviour.

As I have walked in faith as a reborn Christian, I have learned that when God take's us through something to beaware because some one is going to be around us that may have a similar promblem and we are to help. That is a resonable service as a Christian. God does not teach us something, for us to keep. He teachs us so we can help others. So let us never be like the chief priest, who was full of envy, and stir up others towards God (refer. Mark 15:10, 11). Let's never think that we are better than others, lets never be high, and mighty, and religious for ourselves, for this would never be of God. God is humble, did He not turn Him self into a man, to save us from the world? God is giving, did He not give His only Son, so that He could have many? God is foregiving did He not foregive us of sin through the blood of the lamb? God is caring, did He not leave us with His word to guide us? God is merciful, did He not allow us to come to His thone of grace to obtain His mercy? God is love, and love is not love unless we can give it away. God is of all these things, and much more, and He made us in His image (refer. Gen. 1:26) so shouldn't we be of those qualities if we are of God? Yes, but know that if we make a mistake, or fall short of God's glory, He still love's us, and He will never take back His grace. He gave it to us, and remember it is only love if you are giving it away. I believe this is why our first two commanments are (1) THOU SHALT LOVE THE LORD THY GOD WITH ALL THY HEART, AND WITH ALL THY SOUL, AND WITH ALL THY MIND. (2) THOU SHALT LOVE THY NEIGHBOR AS THYSELF. Our Churches were not meant to be museum's for the Saints, but are to be God's hospitals for sinners to care for one and another. We can say this is Gods vision; to love thy God, and our mission is to give His love with our's to our neighbor's wether saved or not (refer. Matt. 22:37-39). Love when given away, will never fail us, it never failed God, He gave His love with His Son, and gained many more. Hatred stirreth up strifes; but love covereth all sins (refer. Prov. 10:12). Life giving words will only come from a righteous heart, but only violent words will come from a wicked heart (refer. Prov. 10:11). By loving and giving it to someone else, we are becoming spiritually rich, and this is better than being materially rich. So, as reborn Christians let's try to replace the world's anger with a kind gentle response, and show our love for the only God. This comes from a man that was only about himself and the world, untill Jesus touched him. God can take a no body, and turn them into a some body. If He would do this for me, I know He would do it for you. All we have to do is be willing and obedent to Gods word, try to listen, and get confirmation. If it is God, He will confirm

The first time that we can find grace in the bible is in the book of Genesis, chapter six verse eight. But Noah found grace in the eyes of the Lord. First Noah knew to look to the Lord for grace, second, he obtained it for him and his family, for he listen, and he was obedient to God (refer. Gen. 6:22). The Bible describes Noah as a just man a perfect man of his generation, and that he walked with God (refer. Gen. 6:9) Just here means that Noah had a moral standard for himself, and perfect is talking about a completeness, and I believe Noah's life is a very good example for us all. So if we can listen to the Lord, and be obedient to Gods word and set moral standard's for ourself, and our family, and apply God's word to our everyday life, and keep our eye's focused on the Lord, and His commandments dear to our heart, this is a good start for us to get closer to our completeness, with God, and when we are doing these things of God this is when we can look to the eye's of the Lord for His grace, but we must be patient for His grace to work in our life's, for God's everlasting love for His people is accompanied by infinite patience, and love is made up of two parts, kindness, and patience. So if we are of God, and love is not love unless you give it away, and love is kindness, and patience, so then should we not be kinder to everyone, should we not be patient with other's? Yes we should, because this is were we can start setting our moral standards with love, because love will never fail us. Noah loved God and God loved Noah, and Noah found grace in the eye's of the Lord (refer. Gen. 6:8), and we know that from Genesis chapter six verse nine that Noah was just and up right person why, because he was standing on the Rock his Rock was God, God's work is perfect: for all his ways are judgement: a God of truth and without iniquity, just and right is He (refer. Deu. 32:4), Noah's character was in line with God's character, and I believe to recieve true grace in the eye's of the Lord, we need to line our character with God's, because we can not expect God to do things our way, we want Him to, but the truth is God has a will and a purpose, and a plan, and what we can do first is to seek God by praying, for we as christians will be defeated with out prayer, and if we want more power with God we must have more prayer, if we want much wisdom we need much prayer, second search for God's will through the word of God, when we stay faithful to His word, and we are tring to apply the sword of God to our life He will be faithful and reveal His word to us, in a way that we will understand and always try to pray and to search according to His will, and purpose, I allways tell God I do not know Your plan, but I agree with it. My friend remember that we are saved, given the Holly spirit, and allowed to serve God by His grace. Through our faith, we believe that Jesus died for our sins.

I would like to speak, about a promble alot of us have, by God's grace. This is about our greatest needs. We all feal that our greatest need is to have a big fancy house to live in. We all feal that our greatest need is to have a new fine car to drive in. We all feal that our greatest need is to have the finest clothe's to wear. We all feal that our greatest need is to have alot of money to spend. The truth is we have been handed these standards by man. For if it was from God, our greatest need would be His Son Jesus. So that we could have ever lasting life with Him. So that we would be more thankful. So that we would be more caring. So that we would be more kinder. So that we would be more merciful. So that we would be more humble. So that we would be more understanding. So that we would be more forgiving. So that we would be more giving. So that we would love everyone. Now we all know that we recieve God's grace when we excepted Jesus, and the truth is the greatest need's that man made our standards on, mean nothing without the Lord. Because, we cannot take them with us when we die, but we can be with the Lord. We can take care of His house, and He will take care of ours. His promise to the one's who excepted Him as their Saviour was. In my Father's house are many mansions; if it were not so, I would have told you. I go to prepare a place for you (refer John 14:2). Then Jesus goes on to say in verse six. Jesus saith unto him, I'am the way, the truth, and the life: no man cometh unto the Father, but by me. Jesus does not tell us about the way, nor does He show us the way. He does not even guide us along the way. He says He is the way! Now all we have to do is except the fact that He is the only way. Then by the Holy Spirit He will guide us through life so that we will recieve everlasting life with Him. My friend lets pray in one accord let's agree together. Dear Heavenly Father thank You for covering our sins with Your only Begotten Son, thank You for the way You have provided, thank You for Your grace, thank You for the Holy Spirit that guide us, thank You for the strength to worship and praise only You. And we know that all things work together for good to them that love God, and that it was God's love that gave us His grace, not according to our works, but according to His own purpose, and grace, which was give to us in Christ Jesus before the world began, and we praise You only for that grace for we know even You would suffur the pain of sin so that we would have a chance to recieve the promise of Abraham by our faith, and we just want to be thankful in our hearts. That God has not given us the spirit of fear, but of power, and of love, and of a sound mind, and we pray for the strength and the knowledge to obey your word and keep Your commandments dear to our heart, so that we are ready to do good works, so that we would not speak evil of no one, but to be gentle, and show kindness to everyone, and to stand firm in our faith. To have the strength to confront other's with the spirit of love only. Because we know Your love will never fail us it will only bring Your Grace, and we praise You for that in Jesus Holy Name. Amen.

We know God's grace come's from His love for us. So then you would have to think if we was to love everyone that we could. We would me in the middle of God's grace. This is true, but to recieve God's grace in it's fullness. Is to be more like His Son, and give our love away. To hide His commandments in our heart's, to cherish them everyday. To never force them on another. Yet be an example of them by living them everyday in our live's. Let's try more today than we did yesterday, to make His commandments the standards by which we believe in. Let's build our house's on them. Let's try more today than yesterday to apply them to our everyday life. Then as long as you are tring or, even wanting to do this God's grace will surround you. For God knows that our heart's want to do His will. Even if we stumble, or fall. What we must watch is to not condem ourselves, and fall away from God. This is why Paul wrote in Romans chapter seven verse fifthteen. For that which I do I understand not: for what I want to do, that do I not; but what I hate, that do I. This does not mean to go and sin. He is wanting us to understand the nature of the flesh is to sin, and the Holy Spirit's job is to guide us to do good. Our job as a christian is to fight the spiritual war against the flesh. That is to feed the spirit God's word, and starve the flesh of sin. This is not easy, but when you can stay in the word of God, you are wanting to fight the battle. Beware though, and perpare your heart through prayer for the battlefield. For where God will lead you, He will provide for you. God does not need a bunch of stuffy shirt religious people. Who only care's about their selve's, and what they can get. No, God needs people of the faith that will except His grace, and will work together with Him. Someone who will obey His voice. Someone that is ready to love His Son. Someone that is ready to take the fight to Saint. Someone that is ready to feed the needy. Someone that is ready to clothe the naked. Someone that is ready to help that battered spouse. Someone that is ready to encourage a child to do better. Someone that is ready to teach drug's are wrong. Someone that is ready to teach it is wrong to curse your parents. Someone that is ready to stand firm where God planted them. Someone that is ready to love one and another. Someone that is ready to try to do good for His will and purpose. Someone that is ready to be loved by God, and His Son.

Dear friend, Jesus delivered us, from our offenses, and when God raised him from the dead it was for our justification (refer. Romans 4:25). Now by God's grace I want to share what Paul write's about the results of justification. Therefore being justified by faith, we have peace with God through our Lord Jesus Christ. By whom also we have access by faith into this grace wherein we stand, and rejoice in hope of the glory of God. And not only so, but we glory in tribulations, or trouble times also: knowing that tribulation will produce patience; And patience will build character and hope; And hope does not disapoint; because the love of God has been poured out in our hearts by the Holy Ghost which is given unto us. For when we were yet without strength, at the right time Christ died for the ungodly. For scarcely for a righteous man will one die: yet perhaps for a good man some would even dare to die. But God demostrates His own love toward us, in that, while we were yet sinners, Christ died for us.

Much more then, having been justified by his blood, we shall be saved from wrath through him. For if, when we were enemies, we were reconciled to God by the death of his Son, much more, having been reconciled, we shall be saved by His life. And not only so, but we also joy in God through our Lord Jesus Christ, by whom we have now recieved the reconciliation (refer. Romans 5:1-11). Which is the process of bringing opposing parties or people together. Believers, who are justified by faith and reconciled to God by Christ's victory over sin and death, and we are now to be ambassadors of reconciliation for others (2 Cor. 5:18-20). It was one man that cause sin to enter into the world, which was Adam, and so death passed upon all men (refer Romans 5:12). It was one man that would save us. But the free gift is not like the false step. For if through the offense of Adam many be dead, much more the grace of God, and the gift by grace, which is by one man, Jesus Christ, hath abounded unto many. It was God's plan that Christ die as a substition for sin. So that a christian would have the chance to go to heaven, for enternal life. Because Jesus died for everyone, Christians should make their selve's messengers to take the gospel to everyone (refer. Mark 16:15).

Now my friend I want to share a testimonie with you. I have been visiting this lady she is sixty seven for two years. She lives three hour's from where I live. I go about six times a year. When I go we allway's set and talk about the Lord. As I said: we have been doing this for two years. Well it is December of two thousand and five, and during my visit we were talking about the Lord. When she said: we must do good works to get to heaven. Well I knew that was wrong. But when I went to explain. She got upset and thought I was boasting about what I thought I knew. So when I seen it was upsetting her, I had to stop, and I told her I was sorry. So we niether one said anything more about the Lord. When I returned back home, I could not get this off of my mind. I loved this lady so much. I new I had to tell her the truth. Because this is my job as a Christian, and felt it was the right thing to do. I also new I could only do this out of love. So I wrote her a letter about the truth. Here is what I said: Hi, I truely love you. I want to apologize to you, I never meant to upset you, and I never meant to boast or brag about how much I know about God. I just thought that we was fellowshiping about the Lord. I never meant to brag, because I know nothing without the Holy Spirit to guide me. I'am not even worthy of God, and the truth is none of us are, because of sin, that we are born into. But because God is a foregiving God He give's us our salvation by excepting Jesus Christ as our Lord, our King, our Saviour, it is not for our works, so that no man can boast about it (Ephesians 2:8-9). But when we are saved by the blood of the lamb. We are God's creation, created in Christ Jesus for good works, which God has before ordained that we should walk in them (Ephesians 2:10). But we can not get to heaven by good works. If we could we would not needed. Jesus to die for us. But it was God's grace through our faith we are saved. So then we which be of faith are blessed with faithful Abraham. For as many as are of the works of the law are under the curse: for it is written, Cursed is EVERY ONE THAT CONTINUETH NOT IN ALL THINGS WHICH ARE WRITEN IN THE BOOK OF LAW TO DO THEM. But that no man is justified by the law in the sight of God, it is evident: for THE JUST SHALL LIVE BY FAITH. And the law is not of faith: but, THE MAN THAT DOETH THEM SHALL LIVE IN THEM. Christ has redeemed us from the curse of the law, being made a curse for us: for it is written, CURSED IS EVERY ONE THAT HANGETH ON A TREE (Galatains 3:9-13). Honey this is not about who is right, or who is wrong this is the truth, and I love you so much that I want to make sure that you know it. For God sent not His Son into the world to condemn the world: but that the world through Him might be saved. He that believeth on Him is not condemned: but he that believeth not is condemned already, because he has not believed in the name of the only begotten Son of God (John 3:17-18). Jesus saved us from the works, and when we get to heaven we can just thank Him for it. Love you allways, and remember if we slip and make a mistake, or fall Jesus is there to pick us back up, not to condemn us, but to love us. Love is patience, and kindness, and uncondictional and if we do all thing in Love we will never fail. For love is not love unless we give it away. God gave us His love His only begotten Son. Love Allways Phil.

We as Christians are going to be in situations where we must be slow to speak. Even if we are right. So times we have to say we are sorry, even if we are not wrong. We should be slow to speak (refer. Prov. 15:28). So we will recieve guidance of the Holy Spirit. So that we can do what is right. So that we can give a kind gentle response. So that it does not add fuel to the fire of anger (refer. Prov. 15:1). For if you give a good word it will bring cheer to their heart. (refer. Prov. 12:25). Sometimes we must stop in the middle and walk away to recieve that kind word. This will also give the Lord time to deal with their heart out of His love. So that they will recieve your kind word out of your love. My friend if their is anyone who thinks it is our works that get's us to heaven. I want to say first I love you enough to tell you the truth. These are not my words, they are parts of God's plan. Therefore by the deeds of the law there shall no flesh be justified in his sight: for by the law is the knowledge of sin (Romans 3:20). But to him that worketh not, but believeth on him that justifieth the ungodly, his faith is counted for righteousness. Faith is not a work that can earn you righteousness. Faith is the means through which God can impute the righteousness of Christ to us being of sin. Even as David also describeth the blessedness of the man, unto whom God imputeth righteouness without works, Saying, Blessed are they whose iniquities are forgiven, and whose sins are covered. Blessed is the man to whom the Lord will not impute sin. (refer. Romans 4:6-8) And by him all that believe are justified from all things, from which you could not be justified by the law of Moses (refer. Acts 13:39) Knowing that a man is not justified by the works of the law, but by the faith of Jesus Christ, even we have believed in Jesus Christ, that we might be justified by the faith of Christ, and not by the works of the law: for by the works of the law: for by the works of the law shall no flesh be justified. (refer. Gal. 2:16). I am crucified with Christ: nevertheless I live; yet not I, but Christ liveth in me: and the life which I now live in the flesh I live by the faith of the Son of God, who loved me, and gave himself for me. I do not set aside the grace of God: for if righteouness come by the law, the Christ is dead in vain, died for nothing (Galatians 2:20-21). But Jesus never died for nothing, it was for you and I. So that sin would not have dominion over you for you are not under the law, but under grace (refer. Romans 6:14). Being justified freely by his grace through the redemption that is Christ Jesus (refer. Romans 3:24). Now when we get to heaven we will be judged by fire for rewards based on our service for Christ. Every mans work shall become evident: for the day shall declare it, because it shall be revealed by fire; and the fire shall test every man's work of what sort it is. If any man's work endures which he has built thereupon, he shall recieve a reward. If any man's work shall be burned, he shall suffer loss; but he himself shall be saved; yet so as through fire. (refer 1 Cor. 3:13-15). Such a one does not suffer the loss of his salvation, but the lost of reward. There are many more verse's as I have wrote, which is great, but they all lead us to this. Jesus saith unto him, I am the way, the truth, and the life: no man cometh unto the Father, but by me (refer John 14:6). Jesus don't tell us the way, nor does he say He will show us the way. He don't even say He is going to guide us through the way. He says: He is the way! And all we have to do is to except the fact He is the way.

My friend we all must never try to be satisfied with just a little of God's word, or what we would concerned enough to get by. For God's grace is new everyday, for when we can stay faithful to study the word of God. This is when God stay's faithful and reveals the scriptures to us. Even more so when we can pray over the word, and be trying to apply it to our every day live's. We will begin to mature in the lord. We also should consentrate on becoming spiritual minded. So that we are able to judge all things (refer. 1 Cor. 2:15). This mean we are able to judge both earthly and heavenly things. We can now discern what is of the the gospel and salvation. We can discern wether a man truely preachs the truth of God. Thats why we stay in God's word. For who has known the mind of the Lord, that he may instruct Him? But we have the mind of Christ (refer. 1 Cor. 2:16). This tells us we as christians possess the Lord's own understanding, that is, His thoughts, His opinions, His judgements, His plans, and so on. Because he answers his question at the end of the verse. We have the mind of Christ, who the Christian. We must know that we need understanding or to be instructed. If we was going to meet a man. We would have to have directions. If we do not have instructions how to get there, what are we? Lost. This is why we are instructed by God through his word. What we need to do, and to know. If not we are what? Lost. This is why the Leaders encourage us all to stay faithful to studing our BIBLE. So when the time come's. We are prepared, and have the Basic Instruction's

Before Leaving Earth. This is why we stay seeking, stay searching, and never just settle for a little. So when we are saved by Christ it will not only effect our heart, it will also effect our mind's. This is why Paul encouage the Philippains to be likeminded, having the same love, being of one accord, of one mind (refer Philippians 2:2), This is Gods plan to come together by His grace, and to work together with God. God is not going to make you do anything. We must work with Him to accomplish his plan though us. Because He is not a controlling God. We have all heard someone say; if God did not want me doing this. I would not be doing this. That is a lie. God will not make you do anything. He will only give you choice's to make, and even if you make the wrong choice. He still loves you the same. God does not change. Especially just because we make a mistake. His nature, and character is allways the same it will never change, because of us. Please keep that with you through all you do. Now we was just talking about being spiritual minded, and that it will come as you mature in the Lord. One thing that can help us is turn promblems into confession. I mean confess our faults to one another so that we may be healed (refer. James 5:16). Also the more we all become spiritual (which is God's plan). We must be aware of our brother, or sister in the Lord. If we hear, or see, or know that one of us have been overtaken in a fault or, by some transgression, which means a violation of God's law. We as christian's being of the spiritual must help them to be restored to their former moral self. We must be careful. We must confront, but only out of love. We must be kind, gentle, that is have courtesy, and consideration. For what they are going through. We must also consider ourselves when helping. Keeping constant watch over our own lives. So that we would not be morally dragged down as we help deal with the sin of our brother, or sister. We as Christian must learn to bear one and anothers burdens. So that the law of Christ may be fulfill (refer. Galatians 6:1-2) Mutual bearing of others' moral burdens helps a person to get better, and to see the promblem's in their self. We should pray that God will give us the wisdom to help, and constantly lift them up in prayer. I also feal that it is very important to have the prayer warrior's fasting and praying for the one that needs help, and the one's that are helping. We must allway's remember we are working together with God (refer. 1 Corinthians 3:8-9). Keep this with you, and hold it deep in your spirit, and your heart. For you are Christ's; and Christ is God's (refer. 1 Corinthians 3:23). If we can hold onto that all things are possible to the one's that believe in Christ Jesus, and we will allways belong to Him. To stay more spiritual is to have more Christians around us. We must encourage one and another to do better as a husband, or wife. We must encourage one and another to be a better Father or Mother. We must encourage one and another to be a better son or daughter. We must encourage one and another to be more spiritul. We can only do this out of love. Love is the main tool for any Christian to use in anything we do. Because love will not fail us. When we all come to God to except Jesus. We are usually a mess. That is why alot of us come to the Lord. To get our live's right. This is why we need to stay focus on encouraging one and another. So that we can try to do better today then we done yesterday. When we are tring to do better today then yesterday. We will get better one day at a time. You will experience God's grace is new everyday. The longer we do this. The more we will grow in Christ. Then we will grow into Ambassadors for Christ. For Christ reconciled us to God (refer. 2 Corinthians 5:20). Now it is our job as Ambassadors to reconcile God's people to Him. Reconciliation is the process of brining opposing parties or people together. See we were seprated from

God by sin. Jesus came and died for sin and then God raised Him from the dead to bring us back to Him. Jesus had to become sin for us. So that we might be made the righteousness of God in Him. (refer. 2 Corinthians 5:21). Please understand my friend, I know that I repeat things over and over. But if you are like me. We need to hear things more than once, So we can remember, and be able to understand. How to apply it to our everday life. This book is to help reborn Christians. The truth is I never got it the first time I heard something, or I just foregot, or I just did not apply it to my life. But if we do not apply we will not grow. By being Amassabors for Christ we should be growing, and that is God's plan. For God has not given us the spirit of fear; but of power, and of love, and of a sound mind (refer. 2 Timothy 1:7). Power is our ability to accomplish whatever He wills us to accomplish. Love is kindness, patience, and unconditional no matter what. Having a sound mind is a disciplined mind. Please Let pray.

Dear Heavenly Father we thank You for Christ with out Him none of this is posseble. But because of Him all things are possible. We just pray for the strength and knowledge to do better today than we did yesterday. That we would be more humble today than yesterday. That we would be slower to speak today than yesterday. That we would be quicker to hear today than yesterday. That we would be faster to pray today than yesterday. That we could help reconcile your people with you more today than we did yesterday. That we could just be a better Christian today than we was yesterday. And we pray that You would bless us were we need it the most. We praise Your Holy name, and give You all the honor and glory. We praise You for not giving us the spirit of fear, we praise You for the power to accomplish Your will. We praise You for Your love, for it is kind, for You have shower patience. We praise You for You have proven Your unconditional love. When You gave us Your Son. Thank You. You are truely an amazing God, and the Father of Jesus. We give You all the glory, for You are so worthy. And we ask all things in Jesus Holy name. Amen.

It is God's unmerited favor and love that lead Him to instore in us the abilty to be thankful. We just don't allways use it the way He intended. Friend, we all are thankful when He give's the good. When we start to recieve a little bad, we start to rebukeing it. Instead of learning from it. I know it is hard to give thanks when we have lost a job, or our car brakes down, or what ever may go wrong. God's word say's in every thing give thanks (Refer. 1 Thess. 5:18). It is not that we have to be thankful for the bad. It is to give thanks to God showing that we trust Him to bring some good out of our bad. That is to know when we are in the middle of the trouble, that God is going to see us through it. We just cannot let our emotions lead us into a wrong decission. We need to try to be patient, and faithful to God, and trust that He can take our bad and turn it into good. God's eye's are upond the faithful of the land, that they may dwell with Him, the one that walks in a blameless way, he shall serve God (Psalm 101:6). I believe when we are truely thankful to the Lord for what He done for us. That's when we start being faithful. We realize that God's grace brought about our faith in Jesus, which produced love in our heart, which gives us trust in Gods, which will maintain your confidence in God. My friend being thankful is being faithful. Because God cannot give us new unless we are thankful for what we already have. If we have very little, yet we are thankful. We are proving that we trust God, and that we are putting all of our confidence in Jesus. That He is our Saviour. That He is the only way back to God. That alone is enough for us all to be thankful for. See if we didn't have Jesus, or the word of God their would be know directions, and with out directions their is no way. It is simple without directions, no matter where you are going you would be lost. But if we keep our eye upon the Lord. He will be our way, and He shall take us to the Father (refer. John 14:6). We should always try to be thankful, and be content with the things we already have, for He has already said; I will never leave thee, Nor forsake thee (refer. Heb. 13:5). When we can hold tight to that fact "He will never". We may boldly say, The Lord is my helper, and I will not fear what man can do unto me (refer. Heb. 13:6). My friend we should expect to work with the Lord, and allow Him to help us. We as Christians are being disobedient when we don't listen, or when we listen and don't do it. God has a plan we can not argue with faith. By faith we must agree with God's word, that is so we are being obedient. As we walk in faith we should begin to understand the abilty of Gods word to perserve and mature our live's as Christians as we go through our trials. We can not look at tragedy as a curse from God. But we could look at trials of being the means of which God's blessings could come. Now when we can stand strong in faith, and believe that God is going to get us through our trial's, and we get the victory over our trials. This is when God blessings will come. It is His promise (refer. James 1:12). God does not want us to run from our prombles. He would rather us work through our prombles and mature from them (refer. 1 Peter 1:6-7). He does promise to provide us an escape if our testing becomes unbearable to us (refer. 1 Cor. 10:13). But we should try to remember (James 1:12). Than choosing (1 Cor. 10:13). The reason for this, and why God allows our trials in our live's. That He might humble us, and that He might prove us, to do good at the latter end (refer. Deut. 8:16) This is why God tell us through His word. Be a doer, and not hearers only, deceiving our own selve's (refer. James 1:22). Because

Jesus tell's us this: Not everyone that saith into me, Lord, Lord, shall enter into the kingdom of heaven; be he that doeth the will of my Father which is in heaven (refer Matt. 7:21). Just saying Lord, Lord is not enough to save the unbeliever apart from true repentance and faith. But we that are truely saved will be the one that want's to do God's will, and live for His purpose. Now God's will, I have already explained in this chapter, it is to what. Love the Lord thy God with all thy heart, and with all thy soul, and with all thy mind (refer. Matt. 22:37). Now to start to live for his purpose is to begin right here. Thou shalt love thy neighbor as thyself (refer. Matt. 22:39). And who is my neighbor? Well Jesus said it like this. A certain man went down from Jerusalem to Jericho, and fell among robbers, which stripped him of his clothing, and wounded him, and departed, leaving him half dead. You see from Jerusalem to Jericho it was and old winding dirt road that droped off three thousand, and three hundred feet in about seventeen miles, and their was alot of big rocks on the side of it, and if someone was to scream out for help really no one would be able to hear you. So it was a good place for robbers to ambush someone. And by chance there came down a certain priest that way: and when he saw him, he passed by on the other side. And likewise a Levite, when he was at the place, came and looked on him, and passed by on the other side. But a certain Samaritan, as he journeyed, came where he was and when he saw him, he had compassion on him, And went to him, and bandaged up his wounds, pouring in oil and wine, and set him on his own beast, and brought him to an Inn, and took care of him. And on the next day when he departed, he took out two denarii, and gave them to the innkeeper, and said into him. Take care of him; and whatsoever thou spendest more, when I come again, I will repay thee. Which now of these three, do you think was an neighbor, unto the man that fell amoung the robbers? It was the one that showed mercy, and we must do that likewise (refer. Luke 10:30-37). Our neighbor could me anyone that is in need of anything, and Jesus just wants us to help them, and to love them, without prejudice, or partiality. And when we do this we are not only loving our neighbor as ourself. We are proving that we love God with our whole heart, and this is His will and purpose for us. When we can begin to understand to put this first God's grace will show us the rest. Now our Lord Jesus Christ himself, and God the Father, which has loved us, and has given us everlasting consolation and good hope through grace. Comfort's our hearts, and will stablish us in every good word and work (refer. 2 Thess. 2:16-17). Let us therefore come confidently unto the throne of grace, that we may obtain mercy, and find grace to help in time of need (refer. Heb. 4:16). Wherefore we recieving a kingdom which cannot be shaken let us have grace, whereby we may serve God acceptably with reverence and Godly fear (refer. Heb 12:28). Be not carried about with various and strange teachings. For it is a good thing that the heart be established with grace; not with foods which have not profited them that have been occupied therein (refer. Heb. 13:9). But he giveth more grace. Wherefore he saith, GOD RESISTETH THE PROUD, BUT GIVETH GRACE UNTO THE HUMBLE (refer. James 4:6). So then we should submit ourselve's therefore to God. Resist the devil, and he will flee from us (refer. James 4:7). Likewise you husbands, dwell with them, with understanding to knowledge, giving honor unto the wife, as unto the weaker vessel, and as being heirs together of the grace of life; that your prayers be not hindered (refer. 1 Peter 3:7) Likewise, you younger, submit yourselves unto the elder. That all of you be subject one to another, and be clothed with humility: for GOD RESISTETH THE PROUD, AND

GIVETH GRACE TO THE HUMBLE (refer. James 5:5). But grow in grace, and in the knowledge of our Lord and Saviour Jesus Christ. To Him be glory both now and for ever. Amen (refer. 2 Peter 3:18). Grace will be with you, mercy, and peace, from God the father, and from the Lord Jesus Christ, the Son of the Father, in the truth and love (refer. 2 John 3). May Gods grace be with the one's that believe in His Son. Please my friend, lets pray together, lets be one accord, and touch and agree. Dear Heavenly Father, we give thank's for what your Son had to endure to give us your Grace. We give thank's for your Sons love for us that produced your Grace. We give thank's that your Son bared our sins in His own body. So that we would have a chance to recieve your Grace. We give thank's that your Son came to save the world, not to condemn it. We give thank's for the teachings of Christ from your word. We give thank's for by His stripes we are healed. We give thank's that your Son, saved us from the curse of the laws. We give thanks that we recieve the victory through our Lord Jesus Christ. Giving thank's always for all things unto God and the Father in the name of our Christ Jesus. Prasing only you for all these things that your Son done for us. We praise you for your loving-kindness for it is better than life it self. And we pray that we praise only you for the rest of our days. Let all the honor and glory be yours, for the spotless lamb, your Son, our Saviour Jesus Christ. Please allow us to serve only you by your grace. Please allow us to recieve your grace in our heart's, so that our minds does not decieve us. Please help us to be more humble, slower to speak, quicker to hear, and faster to pray more today than yesterday. And we trust you to help us become a better Christian today than yesterday, and we give all the glory in Jesus precious name. Amen.

I have been giving a testimonie after each chapter. Because I feal lead to do so. The truth is I couldn't wait to write this chapter, and to tell my testimonie about Gods grace for my family, and friends. But I have learn by God's grace to be more patient, and I encourage everyone to try to be a little more patient today than you where yesterday. For kindness and patience will produce a love in your heart that will help you to serve God with your whole heart. That is to be doers of the word of God. So that we do not decieve ourselve's. That is to apply Gods word to our everyday life. To beable to turn to it in every circumstance. To know that we can trust Him allways. To know that our trials are to rebuild our faith in Him, and to bring us closer to His charcter. To be more spiritual minded. To have Jesus' thought's, opions, and plan's, and so on. This is now January two thousand and six. My father has went onto be with the Lord two years ago. I really don't want to say he died. Because now he lives on. That is one good thing about knowing your loved ones are saved. They only die once. Becaused if we are not saved and our sins covered by the Lord. We will die twice. That is, we will die pysical and then spiritual. I promise we only want to die once. My father was what you could say, was a good old boy. He like to drink his beer and carry on. But he took care of his family, he loved us. I never told no one this. But when I was a young boy my father and his two brothers was my hero's. I watched everything they did and I taught when I grow up I want to be just like them. When I got old enough I started to smoke cig. then I tried marijuana then when I got older I began to drink beer, and the older I got I kept on trying harder and more dangerous drugs. But now as I have been faithfully walking with the Lord for two year's now. Which alot of people concider just a baby in Christ. But, God has a plan, for I believe the Lord choose to grow me up fast as a reborn Christian to help other reborn Christians. With the promblems we all go through at first. The Lord has shower me live's of four generations of men. It start's with my father's dad which is my Grandfather. He was a strick man that drank alcohol and smoke cigarettes and I'am shure you didn't want to mis up or do anything wrong. Because he had a temper. But now I never saw that side of him. He had allway's controlled it around the children. Now he was what you consider a good old boy. He went to work everyday and he was not what you consider a trouble maker and he took care of his family with the help of my Grandmother. He never did drugs or nothing like that. His family was from Kentucky. My father was his first born child. When my father was about ten years old they moved to a little town call New Richmond outside of Cinti. Where my father went to school and met my mother. Now my father growed up knowing how to drink achol and cig. Because he seen his father doing it and he even tried marj., but he didn't care for it. But he was what you would consider a good old boy too. Except he was a little more crazier than my Grandfather. He would go out and drink with his friends and they would get in fights together. They were not scared of anything and would probably try anything once. But he too took care of his family with the help of my Mother. Now his dad was in his sixty's when he came to meet the Lord, and my father was fifty eight when he came to meet the Lord. Now I have gave my testimonie how wild I was and it was probably ten times worst than anyone of their stories. Now I was fourty two when my father help lead me to the Lord. I was his oldest, but I was the last of his children to come to the Lord. But I love what the Lord said. The last shall be first and the first shall be last. But now what we can see here is. That as each generation of man came up each one add something more worst to the situation. Either with their behavior or the drinking or the drugs. Now by God's grace he had mercy for my Grandfather. Then he gave it to my father and as I sit and look back. God had help my father to become my best hero ever. Because now he was more loving, he was more merciful, he was more humble, he was more caring about others. He just love sharing his testimonie. How God gave him a truck driver His grace. It was God's love for my father that turn my father and his whole family around to a better life serving the Lord. Now what we can look at here is that my Grandfather had come to the Lord at the age of sixty eight. Then my father had come to the Lord age of fifty eight and I was fourty two. Now the fourth generation of men is my son and last year two thosand and five he was seventeen and he gave his life to Christ. Now I have never been so moved in all my life. One Sunday we were at Church and I had my hands to the Lord and my head was down. This was during worship. Well I looked up and right in front of me was my son and he had his hands to the Lord. That brought me more joy than I can even explain. Just knowing he had a chance to begin to know the Lord at seventeen. Just knowing he had the best chance of breaking the tradition of men in our family. What I mean is now I have a good possibilty of teaching him with the help of the Lord. That it is not ok to grow up and only think about yourself, and drinking and druging, and so on. Because remember each generation of man would add something, to make the party better. What scare's me the most is the drugs now day's are way more potent than when I used them. Now he has the best chance to break this curse, and raise his children knowing the Lord. Now we must say: Is't the Lord Good? Yes, he can take nothing an turn it into something, He can take bad and make it good. Now I'am not condemning them they are still my hero's and they allway's will be. Because they did what they had to do to get it right by God grace. See it was God's love, and grace that laid my father down twice before my father would look up. But God never gave up on him. So if any of this sounds like your family never give up hope. Stand strong in your faith and know all things are possible to those who believe in the Son of God. Allways remember we cannot live our live's to be more merciful, and we cannot live a righteous life, apart from God's mercy, and grace. So glory to the Lamb of God. For He paid the price in full. For He fought the battle, and won. For He is the Son of God His name is Jesus, and by His stripes we are healed, and now we have a chance to live with Him forever in Paradise. By God's mercy, and grace. It is God's gift, and you didn't even have to be good to recieve it. But when you do recieve grace pray that the Lord will help you be better today than yesterday. You see my friend, my whole life I believed I had to earn grace. I thought I had to change before I went to Church. Until one day when every thing else failed my father of tring to get his hard headed son into Church. He tricked me and said: would you come to Church, me and your mother are going to reniu our wedding vows. I said: yes I would go to church for that. Not knowing Jesus had a plan, and that was the day the Lord lifted the blinders off of my eye's, and I recieved my divine appoint, and my life change from that moment on. So now you all can see why my father is my hero, and I give all the honor and glory to God for my hero. May God's Grace be with all that believe in His Son, forever and ever. Amen.

Let me now leave you with and encouraging word from the Lord to be a doer of Gods word. Love God and put others first, love your nieghor as your self, never worship anyone other than God, never take the name of the Lord in vain, honor your father and mother, do not kill, steal or bear false witness. Now if we have, we must go to the Lord in repentence and ask for foregiveness. But never do one intentionally and say well I will just repent, for that is willfully sinning and there is no sacrifice for that (refer. Heb. 10:26). Please my friend, we must allways remember to try not to fill our plate to full to where we cannot focus on the Lord. Because He never intended on person to do it all. He even give Jesus deciples to help, and He gave man a woman to be his wife and to help. Their is no I in team work, and if we just do what God has called us to do, we all will be working together to have God's will done on earth, as it is in heaven. Stand strong in your faith and allow God grace to take it's place in your life, and your life will change forever and ever. Amen. Now my friend lets all remember God give's grace unto the humble (refer. Proverbs 3:34). So lets all pray to be more humble to day than we was yesterday, and God's grace will be new every day. So when the Lord calls us to do something for Him let's not say whom am I. Let just remember the Lord said He will always be with us even untill the end (refer. Matt 28:20), and always remember Christians are not lucky. They are Blessed.

Satan

Satan was originally created as one of God's highest angel's, possessing all angelic attributes. His name was Lucifer this is actually the Latin designation for the morning star (Light-bearer), in Hebrew it means the "bright one." Now Satan led angels in a rebellion. He is described as the originator and chief practitioner of sin (refer. 1 John 3:8). He is refer to as that wicked one (refer. 1 John 5:18). He is a thief and destroyer (refer John 10:10). He is a deciever (refer. Rev. 12:9). He is a murder and liar (refer John 8:44). He is the accuser of the bretheren (refer. Rev. 12:10). Satan's activities to this day is opposing the will and the work of God. Satan is tring to copy the work of God with intent to decieve, to try to destroy all that is good. But a Christian can overcome Satan when they can remember the basic's. Which is Jesus is greater than the Devil (refer. 1 John 4:4), but a Christian must still have healthy respect for the enemy; even as the archangel Michael would not confront Satan except in the name of the Lord (refer. Jude 9). Yet a wise Christian will examine carefully their life and they should avoid the situations where they would most likely be tempted (1 Thess. 5:22). Now if a Christian is going to resist the Devil, they can only do this by submitting to God (refer James 4:7-10). Also a Christian should always be prepared for the battle, and if there is going to be a battle you must have armor, so we all need the whole armor of God (refer. Eph. 6:13-17). A good Christian can find great comfort by knowing. As the morning star goes away fast before the rising sun, so Satan, the angel of light, will be banished to outer darkness by the coming of the Son of God.

God created angel's as spiritual or heavenly being's. God sends His angel's as special messenger's or helper's to human being's. Angel's are not to be establish as the same as God Himself, since He created them (refer. Ps. 148:2, 5). They serve under His direction and obey His commands (refer. Ps. 103:20). Angel's focus their efforts on delivering God's messages to us (refer. Luke 1:13), allway looking out, and protecting God's people (refer. Dan. 3:28). The angel's love praising the name of the Lord (refer. Ps. 103:20-21). Before the creation of the wold, there were certian angles who revolted against God and were cast out of heaven. The ringleader of this revolt was Satan (refer. Rev. 12:7-9). Another of these fallen angels is Abaddon or Apollyon, "the angel of the bottomless pit" (refer Rev. 9:11). So if Satan can convince God's angels to revolt against Him should we not be very carefull? Yes, one of Satan's trick's has been that he does not exsist. Why? Because we cannot respond to something that is not there. Because we cannot fight something that is not there. Now if Satan convince's us he does not exsist. He has a better chance of deceiving us from God's work and will. He will say it's ok to have immoral sex. It's ok to be mean to your parents. It's ok to lie and steal. It's ok to do to other's as they would do to you. It's ok to only look out for ourselves. It's ok to take God's name in vain. It's ok to kill. It's ok to commit adultery. It's fun to drink everyday. It's fun to do drugs every day, now if he can convince us of these two things. He knows all the other things will fall right into place. He will now have his blinders over our eye's. He will be working us like a pupet on a string. Have us doing every thing against God, without us even realizing. Unless we know God's word. Then we know Satan as a liar, deciever, thief, murder, and destroyer of all which is good. He wants us to believe that we are not worthy of God. Which that is true because of sin (Refer. Romans 3:23). But we can cover that sin by the blood of Jesus who die for all sin (refer. John 1:29) Being justified without any cost by God's grace through the redemption that is in Christ Jesus (refer. Romans 3:24). Satan wants to lead us out of our mean's. Planting the seed that it will be ok. Satan knows if he can get us out of our means, he will beable to set in an destroy. What we want to realize is not to go along with it will be ok. We can begin with understanding that it is not ok to buy everything we think we got to have on credit. Now Satan want's us to buy everything on credit, and once we max out, he loves it. Because now he knows the first thing that is going to hit us is worry. Then when we are worrying how to make end's meet. He hits us with stress, and without us even realizing he brings anger into this mess. Why can we say this is the work of Satan? Because this is the opposite of what God's word say's. Jesus exact word's are: It is more blessed to give than to recieve (refer. Acts 20:35). So if we are recieving things that we think we must have on credit, and we are not paying it off in thirty days, or less. We have stepped out of our means, and away from our blessings. We cannot even afford to tithe which is ten percent, and this is to come first. Now if Satan can accomplish this he now has us were he want's us. He can begin to divide and to destroy. Now he want's to make us believe that God is not even there for us, or we would not be in this mess. When it was him that lead us down this path. So now he has got our eye's off of the Lord, and on our promblem's. So right their he has now divide us from the Lord and our blessings. For Jesus said: Give, and it shall be given unto you; good measure, pressed down, and shaken together, and running over, shall men give into your bosom. For with the same measure that you use with that it shall be measured to you again (refer Luke 6:38). My friend we cannot give when we owe it all out. We cannot not sit and worry about tommorrow when we are not focused on today. We cannot live longer by worring, it is just the opposite. We will die sooner from worry and stress. This also will relate to having little faith. When we should have total confidence in God that He is going to provide. This is why Jesus tell's us; Therefore do not worry about tomorrow; for tomorrow shall take thought for the things of itself. Sufficient unto is the trouble thereof (refer. Matt. 6:34). What Jesus is wanting us to know is that God is going to provide, so do not worry about tomorrow, for each day has it's own trouble's and challenges. But, that we as Christians should beable to handle the promblems of today responsibly without worring about the promblems of tomorrow. Then our priority is spiritual, and God will take care of the material things, for where God lead's us, He will provide for us, if we seek Him first (refer. Matt. 6:33). See my friend we must realize both sides of the fence. We must know God's word, and that God is good and allways good. That God never intended us to worry or to stress out over anything. God never intended us to to be angry or confused. But when we are in debt. We will worry. We will stress. We will become angry with our children. We will be arguing with our spouse, and the next thing you know we are heading for divorce court. Now Satan's plan has been put into effect. He has took your eye off of the Lord, and has began to divide. Because he wants to destroy all that, which is good. He want's to keep you from God's promise's. He want's us to divorce each other. Why? Because he can work his plan alot easier against us if he divide's us (refer. Matt. 12:25). For their is power in number's. I mean the more of us their is praying for one and another and fighting the spiritual battle. The stronger we become in Jesus' name. It is evident through out the New Testament that Jesus defeated Satan by the capture of soul's from him, and that the Lord's power's over demon's were proof enough that he was the Messiah. The Lord tell's us, His grace is sufficient for us: for His strength is made perfect in weakness. Then we should most gladly glory in our weakness, that the power of Christ may rest upon us (2 Cor. 12:9). My friend we all must know Satan is a powerful opponent. We must also know do not even atempt to take the fight to him without the whole armor of God and in Jesus' name praying (refe Eph. 6:13). Without prayer God's armor is inadequate to achieve victory over Satan. Praying always with all prayer and supplication in the Spirit, and watching thereunto with all preseverance and supplication for all saint's (refer. Eph. 6:18) We must be aware on every occasion, that is when Satan attacks. We must pray not just for ourselves but for all saints, for spiritual combat is both individual and for all saints. We as Christians should know. Even though we live in a body we do not fight according to human standards. We as believers should conduct spiritual warfare, by casting down or destroying of any false imagination or any false arguments that anyone may raise against the knowledge of God. We should allways be tring to bring into our mind every thought to the obedience of Christ (refer. 2 Cor. 10:3-5). And having in a readiness to punish all disobedience, when our obedience is fulfilled (refer. 2 Cor. 10:6). Paul is explaining that we cannot talerate disobedience, or over look it. That there should be consequence's, not of evil, but out of love.

We as Christians have a question to ask the world. Is Satan real? Well "Satan" means resister, or opposer. Lucifer was one of the perfect spirit son of God's. Who acted upon an improper desire and became Satan the Devil. The Bible describes this as a self-corruption. By each one of us by being tried, by being drawn out and enticed by their own desire. Then the desire, when it has become fertile, gives birth to sin; in turn, sin, when it has been accomplished, brings forth death (refer James 1:14-15). What we as Christians want to beaware of is. Our trials and temptations may appear the same, and what may start as a trial may develop into a temptation, if not properly answered by the word of God. Anything that appear's in our life can be answered by the word of God. If we choose to search for it, and apply it to our everyday life. This is our choice to make as a Christian. We must know Satan is real, and that he has a desirer to sift us as wheat. That he has many snares waiting, and set for us. He has many battle fields surrounding us. Here are the one's that I have had to deal with, in my walk in faith. The first battle field I came to was immoral sex with my girl friend. But God gave me the victory. When I began to apply His word to this matter. I was under conviction of the Holy Spirit, and I went to my Pastor. He recommened to seperate for a season or two. I did, and for six months I seeked God, I stayed in the word of God for three to six hours a day learning all I could. Then I ask God for compformation. I ask God for three things, one was a house for under five hundred a month, second was someone was going to tell me to do this, third was my mother was going to except her. So I will never forget this on a Friday after work my girl friend said: let's just get married. Well I had to think about that, because I never had recieved compformation yet. So I went home that night and like all the other nights I prayed. Well the next morning I'am sitting on the couch and I recieved a phone call it was my sister. She knew I was staying with my mother and she ask me if I want to rent one of her house's, one of her attent's just moved. So I said: how much is it. She said: four Hundred and fifty dollars that even include's electric and water. Then I'am sitting their and my brother out of the blue just stops over, and he said; now and we have a nine month baby girl and every Sunday at

Church the woman argue who get's to hold her first, and the baby just love's everyone of them, and love's the music the worship team sings. Now isn't God good, even though I had been listening to Satan's lie for many year's that it was ok to have sex and not to be married. When I began to listen to God he open the heaven's and poured out a blessing that we could hardly contain, and then gave us the best of them all and her name is Chloe. Can you feel our victory now. My second battle field was the smoking of marjiuna. When the Holy Spirit convicted me of this. I began to reason with him. I said you know that I don't do it that much, and I only do it at home. Then the Lord spoke into my heart, yes and I going to love you no matter what, but just think about how many little children you can help from the money you can save, just look at how much longer you can live. So at that moment I told the Lord I'am weak, please help me. Now it has been over a year and I don't even think about it. The Lord has been gragely giving me the strength to over come these battle's and He has shown me the victory is our's with patience, and one step at a time, and with our love for Him, because He allready loved us. You see my friend these snare's are set because Satan want's to keep us as far as he can from God. He is a liar and the only way we can recieve the victory is in a name. That name is Jesus Christ, and the only way to know the truth is through the word of God, because Satan's lie's and temptations are their, and Satan has no chance against the Lamb of God. So let me encourage you to study the word of God. There are many way's to do that, their are CDs, books, tape's, and the leaders of the Church's, and their is the living Bible, which I consider the Basic, Instructions, Before, Leaving, Earth. I believe alot of us get confused when we begin to read the bible. I know I did, and I also know the enemy wants us to believe that it is to hard to learn and that it will take to long, and he will use confussion, lie's what ever he can do to divide us from the word of God. The last thing Satan want's you to learn is the word of God, because he is the opposer. My friend the truth is from my experience, if we stay faithful to the learning of the word of God. God will reveal the truth through the Holy Spirit through our willingness to want to learn the truth, and God has many ways to get us the truth, but we should try to remain patient, opened minded with the willingness to know the truth. The truth is we as christians need God's word we cannot make it to fit our life style. God never changes, so then we should let Jesus conform us to his likeness, and this can happen from learning the word of God how ever we choose to learn, and we should dilgently seek God through our prayer's by going to the throne of Jesus. Now the bible says to get to the Father we must come with the Son (refer John 14:6), and it also say's to enter into His gate's with thanksgiving, and into His courts with praise: be thankful into Him, and bless His name (refer Psalm 100:4). So if we want to go to the throne room to obtain mercy. We must go boldly or confidently to the throne of grace in the name of the Lord to find help in our time of need (refer. Heb. 4:16). Giving thanks alway's for all things into God and the Father in the name of the Lord Jesus Christ; Submitting ourselve's one to another in the fear of God (refer Eph. 5:20-21). Alway's humbling ourselve's, for God will resist the proud, but giving Grace to the humble (refer. James 4:6). Submit ourselves therefore to God. Resist the devil, and he will flee from us (refer. James 4:7) God will hear the prayers of the humble (refer.). Now my friend I believe these are Gods basic instructions how to get to the throne and how to get our prayers answered if they line up with His will and purpose. Alway's know the longer we walk with the Lord our prayer's will come to meet his plan. For He will conform us if we are walking with Him and listening. We will become more spiritual mind to having a mind more like Christ (refer 1 Cor. 2:16). Which is to have His thoughts, opions, and His plan and so on, and this is his will. We can only recieve the victory over Satan through Jesus Christ and that can only be obtain through prayer.

The word of God fore warns us about the antichrist. Which is the archenemy of Christ. The antichrist receives his authority and power from Satan (refer. Rev. 13:4). He is lawless and deceitful (refer. 2 Thess. 2:3 - 12 and 2 John 7). Characterized as a "beast," the antichrist will appear before the return of Christ to wage war against Christ and His people, you and I (refer. Rev. 13:6-8). However, he will be defeated by Christ and cast into a lake of fire (refer. Rev. 19:20). This is evil, a force which stands in opposition to God and righteousness. This evil force originates with Satan, the archenemy of good, truth and honesty (refer. Matt. 13:19). In the end-time God will triumph over evil, and Satan will be thrown into a lake of fire (refer. Rev. 20:10) Satan want's to lead us into iniquity's. Which is sin, wickedness, and evil. But Jesus taught that evil or iniquity originates in the heart, or from within (refer. Matt. 23:28). Christ redeems believers from their iniquity, purifies them, and sets them apart for His service (refer. Titus 2:14).

Let's stop, and think, and ask ourselves some questions. How should we view the Devil? Prince of this world (refer. 1 Cor. 2:6 John 12:31, 16:11) Do we think of him as real person who tempts people to do wicked things? Yes, the devil is an evil being who opposes God, Jesus regarded Satan as a person and he tempted Jesus with the thing's of the world (Matt. 4:1-10) Jesus also discribed the devil as a murderer and the father of lies (John 8:44). Does Satan merely represent the principle of evil? No, he is as a roaring lion, walketh about, seeking whom he may devour (1

Peter 5:8) Is the devil someone to be feared? No, Because Satan is subject to God's greater power, and we are of God, little children, and have overcome them: because greater is he that is in you, than he that is in the world (1 John 4:4) Christ indwells believers; Satan is likewise the lord of his own followers. But Christ is greater than he who wreaks havoc in the world, So by excepting Jesus Christ who has overcome the world, we recieve the victory through Christ, and God said: don't fear I will fight for you (Deu. 3:22) Should he be dismissed as nothing more than a superstitious notion or a mythological unreality? No, but their will be a day that Jehovah – Jireh "the Lord will provide" His plan and cast the devil into a bottomless pit for a thousand years (Rev. 20:1-3) Does the word "devil" refer to some abstract destructive force in the universe? No, Devil is a title for Satan which emphasizes his work as a liar and deceiver (Luke 4:3)

Could the term simply be a symbol of the evil traits in humans, as many modern theologians claim? No, the devil tempted Jesus, an he will tempt us to with the things of the world, but our job as Christians are to fight the temtations of the world, which is spiritual wickedness in high places. (Eph. 6:12), and the only way to fight spiritual warfare is to take unto you the whole armor of God, so that we maybe able to withstand in the evil day, and having done all, to stand (Eph. 6:13) God's armor is (1) Truth, which is God's word (2) Breast plate of righteousness, which represents a holy character and moral conduct, which would be obedience to the truth, which will produce a godly life, which is righteousness. (3) Preparation of the gospel of peace, a Christian should possess a sense of eagerness, or willingness to advance against the devil and take the fight to him. Such eagerness to contend with Satan comes from the gospel of peace. The gospel gives peace to a believer, freeing them from anxiety though he advance's against such a powerful opponent. (4) The shield of faith, taking God for his word by believing His promises. This kind of trust will protect us, from doubts induced by Satan. (5) The helmet of salvation, is the certainty of salvation, which is God's gift (refer. Eph. 2:8). (6) The sword of the Spirit, which is the word of God. Please remember without prayer this does not work. But with prayer be hold the victory is our's in Jesus name. How does the devil influence mankind today? Devil means (slander) the name describes Satan as slandering God to man and man to God. The former work is of course, a part of his great work of temptation to evil; and is not only exemplified but illustrated as to it's general nature, and tendency by the narrative of Genesis chapter three. But his best influnce is to convince us that he does not exist. So that he can keep us from Christ with his lies, doubt, and excuses, for he is the father of lies (refer John 8:44). He will also try to encourage, or draw us into a foolish, or wrong course of actions, or try to lure with the temptations of the world. He give's us these temptation's in way that they don't sound to bad. First he will start off by saying: It's ok, but if it oppose's the word of God it's really not ok. Now this does not mean if we buy one of his lie's we are going to hell, or that God does not love us anymore. That is another one of his lies. God loves us uncondictional this means no matter what. Jesus died for our sin's. For the one's we have already committed, and the one's we are going to committee. Now this is not to just go and sin, this is simple when we have fallen, and made a mistake we can go to the throne of Jesus and humble ourselves to His mercy and ask for foregiveness, and repent of our sin's. Why because Jesus was not sent to condemn the world, He was sent to save the world (refer John 3:17). Now I believe as a Christian this question is one of the most important one of all. What, if anything, can we do to resist Satan's influence?

First is to rebuke Satan (refer Matt. 16:23). Second is we can submit ourselve's to God. Third is to resist the devil, and he will flee from us (refer. James 4:7). Fourth is to keep in our mind's we as Christians should refuse evil, and choose the good (refer. Isaiah 7:15). Fifth is to know Gods word; Be not wise in our own eyes: fear the Lord, and depart from evil (refer Prov. 3:7). So let's all just focus on knowing inorder for us to be able to resist the influence of the devil is to hate all evil, and to know the truth, which is God's word, for God is always good, and only good, and that we as Christians can resist the devil by knowing that God is in control of our every circumstance, and that He has ordain us to good works (refer. Eph. 2:10), and to become more like Jesus (refer. Romans 8:29), and we all must know. That all things are possible when we truely believe in the name of Jesus Christ of Nazereth. So grieve not the Holy Spirit of God, whereby we are sealed unto the day of redemption (refer. Eph. 4:30). So now we agree we all are born of sin, and we have come to the light, and now we are reborn. So then we need to replace a few things in our live's. Let's start with lying is to be replaced with telling the truth (refer Eph. 4:25). Let's replace sinful anger with righteous indignation, that the devil may not be given any opportunity (refer. Eph. 4:26-27). Let's replace theft with honest work, so that we may meet the need's of others (refer. Eph. 4:28). Lets replace foul language with gracious speech, that it may edify others and not grieve the Spirit (refer. Eph. 4:29-30) Let's replace resentment and wrath with kindness and forgiveness since God has forgiven us (refer. Eph. 4:31-32). These are not my sujustgens, but this is Gods word. Here is some promise's we all can count on, if we believe in Jesus. I will never leave thee, nor forsake thee (refer. Heb. 13:5). This is so that we as Christians can boldly say, The Lord is my helper, and I will not fear what man can do unto me (refer Heb. 13:6). Be complete, be of good comfort, be of one mind, live in peace; and the God of love and peace shall be with you (refer. 2 Cor. 13:11). When a man's way please the Lord, he maketh even his enemies to be at peace with him (refer. Prov. 16:7) For God so loved the world, tha He gave His only begotten Son, that whosoever believeth in Him should not perish, but have everlasting life (refer. John 3:16). Who His own self bare our sins in His own body on the tree, that we, being dead to sins, should live unto righteousness: By whose stripes Ye Where Healed. For ye where as sheep going astray: but are now returned unto the shepherd and overseer of your souls (refer 1 Peter 2:24-25). Righteousness is our faith in Christ. That if thou shalt confess with thy mouth the Lord Jesus, and shalt believe in thine heart that God hath raised Him from the dead, thou shalt be saved. For with the heart man believeth unto righteousness: and with the mouth confession is made unto salvation (refer. Romans 10:9-10).

I choose God first

F or God sent not His Son into the world to condemn the world; but that the world through Him might be saved (refer. John 3:17). These are words we can count on, for God is not the author of confussion (refer. 1 Cor. 14:33) For God will not lie (refer. Titus 1:2). Because God is holy in all His works (refer. Psalm 145:17). So now let me help you, if you are setting their saying; I don't know if I am saved or not. Well did you do what Romans 10:9 said to do? If the answer is yes. Then remember God is not the author of confusion, God cannot lie. For by grace you have been saved through faith; and that not of yourselves: it is the gift of God. Not of works, so that no one can boast. For we are His creation, created in Christ Jesus, for good works, which God hath before perpared that we should walk in them (refer. Eph. 2:8-10). We as reborn Christians must know our salvation is real, and we should be striving to apply the scriptures to our life daily. Yet also to know if we make a mistake don't condemn ourself just learn from it, and repent, and tell Satan he is a liar and the father of it (refer. John 8:44). Any time Satan hits us with a lie. We as Christians must hit him with the truth qotue scripture back to him, but only in the name of the Lord Jesus Christ. When we quite buying his lies we will not fall for his temptations. We will stand strong in our faith in Jesus Christ who gave Himself for us (refer. Gal. 2:20). For God made Him sin for us, who knew no sin; that we might be made the righteousness of God in Him (refer. 2Cor. 5:21). If anyone be in

Christ they are a new creature (2 Cor. 5:17). My friend the truth is we must learn our scriptures so we can have a weapon to fight back against, and we need brother's and sister's that are strong in the word of God, and with the Lord we can go back to the camp of the enemie and take back what was our's. Let's stand together for their is power in numbers. Let's open our eye's and turn them from darkness to light, and from the power of Satan unto God, that we may recieve forgiviness of sins, and inheritance among them which are sanctified or set apart by faith that is in Jesus (refer. Acts 26:18). Lets, please quiet our heart's and just pray. Dear Heavenly Father we give thanks for the love of your Son Jesus, and for the Holy Spirit which guide's us. We give thanks for the word of God, which teache's us about your true love and compassion. We give thank's for the men and women of war, for they are fighting for freedom, as Your Son fought the good fight and won two thousand years ago. They are fighting to protect this Country, because it stands for "In God We Trust." So we want to humble ourselve's to pray a blessing for them and their loved ones back home. We fall to the feet of Jesus to pray that God would provide for their need's, and their heart's desirers. We pray that Jesus would take this prayer to God, and guide and protect them. That Jesus would pray that His Father would give them the victory and bring them home safely to their loved one's. For His grace and riches, for His honor and glory. We want to praise the Almighty Living God the Father of Jesus. For He is the Great Jehovah – Jireh for He will provide. We praise Jehovah - Nissi for the Lord is our banner. We praise the God of Jacob, for He is the God of the people. We praise Yahweh - Rapha for He is the Lord that heals. We praise the Great I AM for being the Father of Jesus our Lord of Lords our king of kings our Saviour. We praise El-Shidie for He is the soul creator and the ruler of the universe, all-powerful and perfect in holiness, and infinite in mercy and grace. We praise Shediea for loving us first. We praise Jehovah for sending His Son to save us from our sins. We praise the Almighty Living God for not condemning us, but saving us through Christ. We come now to humble ourselve's to the throne room to ask of forgivness for our sin's. We pray if any of us have sin in our heart's that You the Almighty would remove the sin, and replace it with the love of Your Son. That You would surround us with Your angels to keep us from the temptations of this world. We pray in Jesus' name for the victory over Satan today. We pray in Jesus' name for chains and boundage to be broken today. We pray and lift up the sick and pray the prayer of faith we humble ourselve's before Yahweh – Rapha to ask for healing according to Your will and purpose, and if it is not meant for healing we accept that. Then we would pray that Yahweh would ease the pain and comfort them with the love of His Son. We pray for the needs of the huricane victumes, and we give thank's for the saint's of God that obeyed Your voice, that You sent to help them, and we lift them all up to You and pray for a blessing and that You would surround them with your angels and protect them all for Your glory. Dear Father God I pray for each reader to recieve wisdom, understanding, and guideness from the Holy Spirit. I pray that the Great IAM would reveal Himself through the love of Christ, and through the word of God. I pray they except Your gift of grace which is Your Son, which is sufficent for their salvation. I pray for their needs and their hearts desirers. I pray for you my friend as you walk by faith as you hope for God's promise's. That you would reconize God's hand through the good times, and through the bad times. I pray that my friends praise God through the bad times as well as the good times knowing they can trust God to get them through any circumstance. I pray for their strength to carry their cross daily in Jesus' Holy name. Amen.

My friend we as Christians must know we have choice's to make, and the longer we walk with God the harder the choice's become. But knowing God's word we can overcome and recieve the victory through Christ. We cannot choose the sensation's of Satan, which is the things of the world. We cannot let our emotions run wild and cloud our judgement on what is right or wrong. We cannot replace the truth of God with tallurance. We cannot let people control us by manipulation. We cannot give into them to avoid the situation, or the confrontation. We cannot replace the truth with a lie to please other's. We as Christian should live our lives accountable to God for our attitudes and actions. This is when God show's us the truth about how we are we don't get mad, but instead we become thankful. We as Christians need to be held accountable, if we are not. God will not begin to mold us to His character. Because we never truely summitted to God's will. We bought the lie and thought we never need to be held accountable. If we don't hold ourselves accountable and grow from it. What will begin to happen is Satan will step in and begin to lie and try to lead a stray. See Satan cannot controll us or hear our thoughts, but what he is good at is when one of God's children falls, or makes a mistake he will step in and lie and tell us God doesn't love you know more He will not forgive that. This is when we can overcome that lie, and begin to fall on the truth. Which is the Lamb of God takes away the sin of the world (refer John 1:29). Jesus was sent as a spotless Lamb to be a good shepherd that's why He will go after the one that is lead off (John 10:10-11). Jesus bared our sin in His own body so that we being dead to sin could live into righteousness: By His stripes we are healed (refer 1 Peter 2:24). See now we are fighting against a lie with the truth. We just tell the truth and it will set us free (refer. John 8:32).

God gave us a conscience to know right from wrong, and we must be very careful not to continueously to egnor our conscience. What will end up happening is our consciense will grow dull or it will become deaden to what is right or wrong. Then that will leave us with nothing more than confussion. Then it is very easy for us to astray or wounder off from the word of God. But when we agnolige our consciense, and what is right. This will build awareness of God deep within us, and we will know what God wants and expects from us. We also should be very careful not to engage in activities that would bother our conscience. This could lead us into temptations causing us to act on our fealings or our emotions. When really we just need to think things through, and follow our heart. For our heart is the center of our personality, and our spiritual life. It was our heart and God's grace that brought us to obtaining our salvation. That gives us the ultimate liberty from sin. We as Christians should continously yeild our will or give up ourselves to God. This will bring us spiritual victory. Because at conversion, one of our best characteristics is that we have the law of God written in our hearts (refer. Heb. 8:10). We want to beaware if we are egnoring our consciense Satan is at 'work using confussion or tring to dull or deaden our consciense to lead us away from the word of God. His plan is to distract, to divide, to devour, to destroy us. Now it doesn't matter if we have been in the word of God for one minute or fifty years. What does matter is that we stay in the word of God daily. For Gods word doesn't deal with confussion, or distractions, or division, or devouring, or destruction,. The word of God simply shows the way and the truth, and when we apply Gods word to our life. We are yielding up ourselves to God's will and He will give us the spiritual victory.

Example: Submit yourselves therefore to God. Resist the devil, and he will flee from you (refer. James 4:7). Ok, first is to submit "meaning" to give into or surrender to anothers authority. This is what took place the day of conversion. Ok, second is to resist "meaning" to work against or actively oppose: to withstand. So when the devil comes to distract we stay in the word and he will flee. So when the devil comes to divide the church or husband from wife or wife from husband or tries to steal our children. We go against his lies with prayer for guideness. We stay in the word for the power of truth. Give thanks unto the Lord; call upon his name: make know his deeds among the people (refer. Psalm 105:1). For his loving kindness is great toward us: and the truth of the Lord endureth for ever. Praise the Lord (refer. Psalm 117:2). This is no matter what trust the Lord. Fight for your husband, wife or children with the truth, being patient, kind, and understanding, yet firm in the word of God. This is true love, and love will not fail us. That is how we can stand against division. Now the devil comes to devour. He could hit us with sickness he did Job. He disired to devour paths of his skin, and limbs of his body (refer Job 18:13). But here is what Job did. First he never blamed God (refer. Job 18:21) Second he stood firm in faith. For he knew that his redeemer liveth, and that he shall stand at the latter day upon the earth: (refer. Job 19:25). Even though Satan was tring to devour Job skin. Job said: yet in my flesh shall I see God; (refer Job 19:26). Not only did Job stand in faith, he proclaimed faith. Shall I see God. He is talking about his resurrection body and that he knows he is going to heaven. That is how we can stand against Satan in the eye of the storm, no matter what the problem maybe. Proclaim our faith and come with thanksgiving in our heart, that we have been redeemed and sealed to the day of redemption (refer Eph. 4:30). And only let God's praises come from our lips

Because His loving-kindness is better than life, my lips shall praise thee (refer Psalm 63:3). When we give God praises it declares our longing for spiritual renewal. This will also bring a hedge up arround us and Satan will not beable to devour. When Satan come's to destroy. We hit him with the power of truth. We are children of God and have overcome them: because greater is he that is in us than he that is in the world (refer 1 John 4:4). Let that therefore abide in us which we have heard from the beginning. If that which we have heard from the beginning shall remain in us, we also shall continue in the Son, and in the Father. And this is the promise that he has promised us, even enternal life. These things have I written unto you concerning them that try to decieve us. But the anointing which we have recieved of him that abideth in us, and we need not that any man teach us: but as the same anointing teacheth us of all things, and is truth, and is no lie, and even as it has already been taught to us we shall abide in him (refer. 1 John 2:24-27). The truth is the word of God will furnish us with knowledge, and which the spirit then makes relevant and applicable in our life. Before Christ was cruiecfied He gave us a promise He said: The Comforter, which is the Holy Ghost, whom the Father will send in my name, he shall teach you all things and bring all things to your remembrance whatsoever I have said into you (refer John 14:26). This is why the word of God is important to us. If we don't read it the Holy Ghost has nothing to bring in remembrance. If we don't read we don't know what Jesus said into us. But please remember if you feal like you don't understand as you read please continue and stay faithful for God will supply the knowledge but it will come from your faithfulness. The word also say's: I give some apostles; and some, prophets; and some, evangelist; and some, pastors and teachers. For the equipping of the saints, for the work of the ministry, for the edifying of the body of Christ. Till we all come into unity of the faith, and of the knowledge of the Son of God, unto a mature man, unto the measure of the stature of the fullness of Christ (refer Eph. 4:11-13) This is speaking about the church each one of us is an entrical part and have been given gifts to further His work and to come together with our faith to share into the knowledge that He has gave to each one of us. This is why we want to be part of a good loving Church and we want to have the whole Armor of God, that we may be able to stand. When Satan attacts to destroy. We can know we did all to stand (refer. Eph. 6:13). That is to say if we know the word. Because that is the only way to victory over Satan while we are on earth. There are hundreds of promise's in the bible and as we learn them we can use them. When satan attempts to destroy beggin to quote the scriptures and God's promise's to us. We simply say it has been written this is the power of the truth. When the tempter came to Jesus, he said if thou be the Son of God, command that these stones be made bread. But Jesus said: It is written, Man shall not live by bread alone, but by every word that proceedeth out of the mouth of God. Now Satan was not happy with that. So he took Jesus up into the holy city and put Him on the pinnacle of the temple. And said: into Him, if thou be the Son of God, cast thyself down: for it is written, He shall give His angels charge concerning thee: and in their hands they shall bear thee up, least at any time thou dash thy foot against a stone. But Jesus said into Satan, It is written again, THOU SHALL NOT TEMPT OR TEST THE LORD THY GOD. Now again Satan takes Jesus up into an exceeding high mountain showing Jesus all the kingdoms of the world, and the glory of them. Then told Jesus all these things I will give to you, if you will fall down and worship me. Then Jesus said to Satan, away with you, Satan: for it is written, THOU SHALT WORSHIP

THE LORD THY GOD, AND HIM ONLY SHALT THOU SERVE. Then the devil leaveth him, and, behold, angels came and ministered unto him (refer Matt 4:3-11). We can see the victory was obtained on each temptation by Jesus using scripture. We can also see how tricky Satan really is. The scripture Satan quoted was from Psalm 91:11-12, but if we was to read on in the scriptures here is what we would find. Thou shalt tread upon the lion and cobar: the young lion and the serpent shalt thou trample under feet. Because he has set his love upon me, therefore will I deliver him: I will set him on high, because he had known my name. He shall call upon me, and I will answer him: I will be with him in trouble; I will deliver him, and honor him (refer. Psalm 91:13-15). So when we read on, it was really the way to get the victory over Satan. Satan even knows the scripture, but to tell the truth is to tell the whole truth. This is a valueable lesson to us. For two reasons to know the scripture's, and to know the importance of telling the whole truth. Because Psalm 91:16 gives us God's promise verse sixteen: With long life will I satisfy him, and show him my salvation. Last was for Jesus to fall down and worship Satan and Satan was going to give him the world, but their was a promble here and Jesus knew. That it was not Satan's to give. The world was created by the Lord THY GOD, and if Jesus was to worship him he would have been saying that he was Lord. But Jesus did not so He proved He was Lord and that He would soon crush Satan. This is why I love this scripture John 14:23 and I qoute, If a man love's me, he will keep my words: and my Father will love him, and we will come unto him, and make our home with him. The promise here is based on love and the obedience to Jesus' word. For the greatest sin is to not believe, while the greatest work is to believe. Satan cannot destroy when we use the words of the Lord's. Christianity can be described in these four words. First is knowing, knowing this, that our old man is crucified with him, that the body of sin might be destroyed from here on we should not be slaves of sin (refer. Romans 6:6). This is to say we have the power to serve Christ instead of sin. Second is reckon which means to take into account or to consider. Likewise reckon, or consider you also yourselves to be dead indeed unto sin, but alive unto God in Christ Jesus our Lord (refer. Romans 6:11). We as Christians should consider all the facts that identify us with Christ and our seperation from sin, and then live our live's accordingly. Third is yield, neither yield or present your members as weapons of unrighteousness unto sin: but yield or present yourselves unto God, as those that are alive from the dead, and your members as weapons of righteousness unto God (refer. Romans 6:13). This is to say in our daily confrontation with sin we should not give in, and to just stay commited to God. Fourth is obey, but God be thanked, though you were the slaves of sin, but you have obeyed from the heart that form of doctrine "pattern of teaching" to which you were entrusted (refer. Romans 6:17). We as Christians should allways be thankful to God, for that will help us to become humble in our own live's, and we should learn the word of God to beable to obey God from our heart's, for the heart is what God will judge. My dear friend let's pray. Dear Heavenly Father we give thanks and we humble ourselves at the feet of Jesus and pray that you would except us as a living sacrifice not according to what we have done, but according to what your Son has done in us. We just pray that you Jehovah – Jireh the Lord that provides will put up your hedges arround our husband's and wive's our children our family members our church our friends to protect and to keep safe from Satan's grasp that you the Great I'am would lead us in your every way as we pray to have the strength and the knoledge to serve Jesus as Ambassadors to Christ to reconcile your people to the Son so that the Son can take them to the Father so that the Son can glorify His Father Who is the ruler of the universe who is the soul creator who is Yahweh – Rapha the Lord who heals. We just pray for peace and your will according to your purpose for your richer and grace. I just pray that each reader would love Your Son and keep His word. So that You would love them and that You and Your Son would make Your home in them, and the Lord thy God would surround them with His angels and we give You all the honor and glory in Jesus' name. Amen.

We as Christians should beware that when we go through a storm wether it be sickness, marital promblems, or trouble with our children what ever the case maybe, and to know that it is not Satan. For he does not have that kind of power. But what he does when we come into the storm is beggin to lie to us. He tells us we are not worthy of God now. But the truth is God might just have set us right in the middle of the storm. But He always set's us right on the rock, the perfect corner stone His Son. To see if we will stand in faith and trust Him, or to see if we are going to just walk arround the promble. Because if we don't deal with it and fall back to the word of God it stay's a promble. God simply ties us to it. Now if we seek God first and deal with the promble and resolve it in a mature and reasponseable manor. We walk straight through the promble to the promise and provision of God. What is His promise, I will never leave thee, nor foresake thee (refer Hebrew 13:5). What is His provision our need's not our want's, but our needs. But seek you first the kingdom of God, and his righteousness; and all these things shall be added unto you (refer. Matt. 6:33). Remember the children of Isareal walked in a circle in the wilderness for fourty years, and most of them died their they never walked straight through the promble. The promble was their murring and complaining. And Mose's never seen the promise land because of his anger. First he killed an Egytian then God told him to smitten the rock. But he smitten the rock twice the second time was out of anger. This does not mean they was not saved. What it does mean is they never recieved the promise. Except God allowed Joshua and Caleb take the one's that where twenty years old and less. I believe it came from their faithfulness and Gods promise to Abraham. The point I'am tring to make is that our promble's can keep us from the promise. But if we are in the middle of the storm on a rock stand in faith with thanksgiving in our heart, and praises from our lips, and watch the storm calm.

Now I want to end this chapter reaching out to this generation about a drug deamon. As I see this generation coming up in the world. I see this drug deamon rainting and raving back in fourth devouring this generation with a urgentcy. They now posses drugs such as crack, meth, herion, cocaine, pain pills, even huffing airisals. Their plan is to devour quickly. For with these drugs it will not take long, and they steal the will to live. For the longer anyone stays on these drugs the less they want to live, they actually want to die. The addiction rules their live. One way to know it is bad they will start lying, then stealing, then whatever it takes. But, now I want to reach out to my generation and encourage each one to go into the eniemies camp and take back our children from these thiefs who's desirers are to devour them. First we need Jesus, second lot's of prayer, third lot's of love, fourth lot's of patience, fifth lot's of strength, sixth lot's of truth. Seventh zero tallarence. First is Jesus as our king, our lord, our personal Saviour. Second our prayers are for everyone that is envoled to decern out good from the bad. To be guided by the Holy Spirit. Remember Jesus said: Ask, and it shall be given, seek, and you shall find, knock and it shall be opened (refer. Matt. 7:7). This is to humble ourselves and ask, for God hears the prayer of the humble, and He will exalt them (refer. 1 Peter 5:6). This is to look first to God to be guided by genuine prayer, for he that seeketh findeth (refer. Matt. 7:8). To knock is to have a fervent prayer "fervent is to have a passionate or very hot prayer" and continue in prayer for those who we are concerned with.Third is love, remember love is not love unless we give it away. Love will never fail us. For God is love and if we abide in love, we abide in God, and God will abide in us (refer. 1 John 4:16). We cannot help anyone without love. Fourth is patience and it will grow from our love. Because the very core of love is patiente and kindness. This is a hard one but the quicker we get it the easer it becomes. Rejoice in our troubled times also, knowing that your troubles will produce patience (refer. Romans 5:3). This is us knowing that God is incontroll of our every circumstance. Our patience will build our character and allow us to experience, hope. Our hope will not disapoint us, because the love of God, is pour into our hearts by the Holy Ghost which is given into us (refer. Romans 5:4-5). These are not my words, but they are Gods. He shows us the way, the truth and the promise. It is our choice if we want to obey or to apply to our live's. That's how great He is. Fifth is strength, Which will only come from the Lord. We can do all things through Christ which strengthen us (refer. Phil. 4:13). This is how we can handle any extreme circumstance, knowing that it is not from us, but it is from who abides in us. That is our true strength, it is His gift to us. We just got to believe, and learn to adapt to the circumstance's of that day, and know that God give's us the strength to be content in all situations. Their are going to be times when strong has to bear the weakness of the weak, not to please ourself. But to please our nieghbor for his good to help build up him. For even Christ never pleased himself; as it is written, THE REPROACHES OF

THEM THAT REPROACHED THEE FEIL ON ME. See the things that were written beforehand were written for our learning, that we through patience and comfort of the scriptures might have hope (refer. Romans 15:1-4). Again He shows us the way, the truth, and here is His promise. But the God of all grace, who has called us unto His eternal glory by Christ Jesus, after that you have suffered a while, make you perfect, confirm, strengthen, settle you (refer. 1 Peter 5:10). Sixth is truth, the truth is what set's us free (refer. John 8:32). The truth will bring us to trust in the Lord. For we can do nothing against the truth, but for the truth (refer. 2 Cor. 13:8). Sometimes the truth hurts the one we are telling it to. But, if we can get them to admit to the truth. This will begin their healing, even though it is along process. They have choosen the way of the truth: thy judgements have I laid before me (refer. Psalm 119:30). It is the truth that comes from our mouth, that shows no injustice in our words, that proves the Lord is walking with us in peace and equity, and we will help many to turn from their iniquity, or injustice (refer. Malachi 2:6). Again the Lord shows us His way and His truth, now here is His promise. Brethern, if any of you do wonder from the truth, and if one turns them back. Let them know, that they which turns the sinner from the error of his way shall save a soul from death, and shall cover a multitude of sins. (refer James 5:19-20). Seventh is no tolerance, we cannot tolerate, or put up with lies, or stealing. We have to confront, but we must do it out of love. If we want it to work, it will also take our patience. We have to wait for the Lord, for He will make the way. So we must stand strong in His word. Then we must pray for every circumstance that come into play, and then the truth will set the captive free. The drugs of to day are very adictive, and when someone become's adicted. We as Christians should do all we can to help get them the treatment they need. But at the sametime we must remember. They have to want our help. If we force it nine out of ten times it will not work. Our job is to plant the seed. It is God's job to water. For we are God's fellow workers with God (refer 1 Cor. 3:8-9). It is simple, duty is our responsibilty, and the results are Gods.

Dear friend I want to plant a seed in your heart to day out of love. I give Satan no glory and want to say the devil cannot make us do anything. But what we can beawe of is when we make a mistake, or we have been running from God, what ever the case maybe. The devil put's his two cents in and plant's a lie, and say's we are not worthy. The truth is we are not worthy, but the devil did not tell the whole truth, so it became a lie. Because it is nothing we say or do. This is the truth. Gods true mirical and His plan that came to pass, or has already happen. Was when Jesus bared our sin's in His body. He became sin, who never sinned. Our sin was transfered to Jesus. By the grace of God it was His first gift. Now the second gift was when God transfered Jesus' righteouness to us. When we believe in the crusifexen which brought the resserrection. When God raised Jesus from the dead. When we truely except and believe and confess it with our mouth. Our confession is turn into salvation, and then all things become possible through Jesus Christ our Lord of Lords our King of Kings our Saviour. The Son of God. Amen.

I was setting in a garage. Some called it a Church. But I had went their to see my father and mother reniue their wedding vow's. As the preacher, peached something happen. He became to me Jesus, not physical but spiritual. I believe the Lord lifted Satan's blinders from my eye's and I had a divine appointment that day, and the Lord used my Father and mother to get me there. As I look back. I can see in the spiritual that the Lord was not afraid to get dirty. Because He got down in the mud so deep to dig me out of that hog pen from Satan's grasp to wipe the mud from my eye's. So that I could see the truth. The reason I say He had to go so deep is I had to be in deep. I was their for fourty two years. But Jesus love's us all enough to come in the hog pen and get us. Our job is simple, just believe. Now I'am a member of Harvest Rain, I'am the Pastor's armour bear I'am the founder of our Men's fellowship Group, and the Lord is using me to write to you. But it was nothing I said or done. It all came from a day I began to believe, and what better place for a painter to be saved but in a garage God does have a sense of hummer. But I known all of this did not come from me. But it did come from who is in me. The week I was saved, and the next week my father died. But if there is anything I learn is that God wasn't done with my father because my father helped our Pastor to get Harvest Rain up and running. And now he live's in all of us, and the Church is growing more and more every week, and we all give God all the glory. As I get ready to close this chapter this is what Harvest Rain Had to say:

Now let's encourage each other, and lets give God the first hour out of everyday. Let's give God the first day out of every week. Let's give God the first dime out of every dollar. Let's then live everyday like it is the first day of the week. Amen

BODY OF CHRIST

The Body of Christ means we are the members of the Body and Christ is the head. We are choosen by God we are given gifts to help the Body of Christ. What we want to realize is our gifts, and to know they will help us to reach out to others. Our gifts will also help us to reconcile God's people to Him through Christ. We are saved by faith through grace, and by salvation we become saints of Gods. Saint means; seperated ones. We as Christians are seperated in two ways. First we are seperated from all that profane and set apart, or reserved for God and His use. Second is we are seperated from evil by Christ, which then makes holy and pure. We as the Church will have to stand firm behind our Pastor in his decisions. Because he is God's overseer of the Church having the spiritual oversight of our Church. His duties are to nurture, protect, and to care for God's saints, or Gods children. As the body we must have fellowship in the gospel to plan and help our pastor. That is to pray allways for him, and to support him finicially, and support the vission that God gave him. Our job is to use our gifts together to allow the body to grow, and to trust God for our sanctifications which means "to be set apart." We as the members of the body need to reconize that the Holy Spirit is attempting to make us holy and spiritual reflecting the character of God, and He use's all things to accomplish His purpose of making us more like His Son Jesus. Even through the good in our life and even through the bad. Now we just need to learn how to except this and grow from this, for we are children of God. Being filled with the fruit that is righteousness, which comes through Jesus Christ for the purpose of glorifying and praising God. The members of the body who are pure meaning "free from anything that damages, weakens, contaminates, or innocent" and without offense before God has divinely developed in him a practical "righteousness" or daily moral life that measures up to God's standards in character and conduct. The ultimate purpose for this righteousness is to glorify God. God's standards can be described in one word love. Walk in love towards your family, friends, emienies, and anyone we come in contact with. We are then not only glorifing God, but we are then being a good example of what Jesus would do. This is also to say if anyone is not living like this don't be condemn but be encouraged, because if we put effort and believe in the Son all things are possible. Each one of us are entrical part's of the body. Wether we be the finger, or the hand. Wether we be the foot, or the toe. We have been called to the body to do something. The first thing we want to remember is to have the right motivation which is "here that word is again" love, and the love for God. Which will give us the strength to accomplish our part. We want to beable to show love towards everyone especially unbelievers. When we show love to everyone we are maginifing Christ (refer. Phil. 1:1-20).

When we say love, we known we are responsible for our happiness. When we say love, we don't let people steal our joy. When we say love, we don't mean rescue, we mean comfort. When we say love, we don't mean give up, or quit, we mean press on, go forward. When we say love, we mean to respond to prombles with respondbilty. When we say love, we don't mean to do things out of guilt. When we say love, we know to set boundaries. When we say love, we know to make consequence's. When we say love, we know to confront a lie. When we say love, we know not to condone stealing. When we say love, we know to understand the possession they have got into. When we say love, we know that we cannot please people all the time. It will just get in the way of our work for the Lord. When we say love, we don't pressure people into what we want. When we say love, we speak the truth out of love. When we say love, we take the high road and walk in love. When we say love, we don't replace the truth with tolerance. When we say love, we don't let anyone control us with manipulation. When we say love, we don't give in to the situation to save the confortation. When we say love, we become encourager's not discourager's. When we say love, we stand in unity for the will and purpose of the Body of Christ. When we say love, it is with our patience and kindness. When we say love, it is unconditctional no matter what. Love is loving thy God with all thy heart, and with all thy soul, and with all thy mind. Love is loving thy neighbor as thyself. I love them that love me; and those that seek me early shall find me (refer. Proverbs 8:17).

In the Body of Christ one thing we can do for spiritual growth is to fellowship. When we share our testimonie's and our walk with the Lord. We bring unity to the body by getting to know one another. Fellowship is when we communicate in love with other Christians, and the whole body will become stronger. Sometimes we as a member of the body will need to confess our faults to one another, so we can be healed. (refer. James 5:16). As we strive to develop a unity of spirit and mind. Remember without fellowship, we cannot live for God. Because if we was by ourselve's their would be no Body of Christ. We must choose to work together for the vision God gave to our Pastor. Only let our conduct be worthy of the gospel of Christ: that wether I come and see you, or else be absent, I may hear of your affairs, that you stand fast in one spirit, with one mind striving together for the faith of the gospel (refer. Phil. 1:27). When we are a memeber of the body we want to focus on our conduct and keep it in unity of one spirit. We should allways be tring to be more humble, patience towards others, and going out of our way to maintain harmony, or peace among God's children (refer. Eph. 4:3). There is one body, and one spirit, even as you are called in one hope of your calling (refer. Eph 4:4). Now this verse say's so much about the body, and if we was reading from a King James Study Bible, and was to read from the study hints they would say; (1) one body – the one body of Christ, which is the Christian Church. (2) One Spirit – the same Holy Spirit who grants the same spiritual life to all believers, (3) one hope – all Christians share the same future, and are headed for the same heaven, (4) one Lord – we all submit to the same divine ruler, which is Jesus. (5) one faith – we all have placed our trust in Christ for our salvation. (6) one baptism – Holy Spirit baptism at the time of salvation (1 Cor. 12:13); and (7) one God and Father – we all that are in Christ have the same God and Heavenly Father. This really show's us we are all called to a Body of Christ and that Jesus is the head of that Body. That there is going to be sacarifice on our part for the well being of that body, and that we all have the same spirit that guides us, or that comforts us if we want it to. We all share a dream about heaven. We all should have faith and trust that Jesus is our salvation, and that there is only one creator, one God, and He is Jehovah the great I'am. Let's pray, Dear heavenly Father we thank you for the wisdom You give as You reveal the mystery of the truth of Christ our Lord of Lords We are so thankful that You would send the Holy Spirit to comfort and to guide, for without the love of Christ and the comfort of the Holy Spirit we would just be lost. But You the great Jehovah - Jireh, is the God who provides. We humble ourselve's and pray for strength to stand by faith on one accord having the same mind, being a memeber of one body to serve one Lord Jesus Christ our messiah, the anointed one, the Son of God, Emmanuel, the spotless lamb we praise You and You only. For You choose us and we love You, for You choose to become man to save us from the sin of this world. You came from Your high throne to show us You cares You came to skull mountain to shead Your blood to cover our sin. To offer us a chance to have enteral life, and all we have to do is except, believe, and confess. You the Lamb of God is our saviour, and we give You all the honor and glory, in Jesus precious name. Amen.

When we are called to the body, we should start seeking God for our calling, and His protection. For as soon as we get on firer for the Lord. The enemy tries to put out our firer. But he cannot, unless we buy one of his lies. We have to stand by faith and be faithful to what God has called us to do. Even if we don't think that it is going to grow. The key to groweth is one word. It is faithfulness. When we can stand in faith and just believe that it is of God, and do what He has called us to do with joy and peace in our heart, not being angry or complaining, because we are asked to do something. But doing it to the best of our abilty and being thankful that God choose us. When we get to this level of our calling, it is us maturing in the Lord. But we need to remember that it will take time and patience, and the willingness to learn, and be lead by the Spirit. But it will come from faithfulness to our ministry. The one thing we really want to understand is if we are in our calling and we fall. The Lord is there to pick us up. This is the biggest benifit to being a Christian. We must know sometimes we must fall to grow in faith, and in trust knowing that the Lord is above all things. That there is nothing that He has not seen, and if we drop the ball in the middle of our ministry. Repent and the Lord will restore it to you. He simply picks the ball back up, and hands it back. Then He sets us up on a new level for even bigger groweth. We all want to remember as we minister beside on an another, we are only as strong as our weakess leak. If our key to spiritual groweth, or muturity in the Lord, is faithfulness, and we are only as strong as our weakess leak. Then we as Christians should watch for the ministies that are struggling, or having troubles, and pray for restoration. But as a body without fellowship we would not know if someone is struggling. So as we have fellowship, we should be discussing our ministies, and what the vision is that God gave us. This is how the body will press on by there faithfulness, and their obedience to God's voice His word, and our prayer's for one another. So today we as Christians should allow the Holy Spirit to develop this character within us. So that we might be blameless before others and not hinder the testimony of Christ. For it is the laborer's of Christ that are worthy of his reward (refer. 1 Timothy 5:18). Let's share some truth of Titus'. Because this is a good example of today. For we ourselve's also were sometimes foolish, disobedient, decieved serving divers lusts and pleasures, in malice "which is a burning desire, or intention to hurt others" and envy, hateful, and hating one another. But after that the kindness and love of God our Saviour toward man appeared. Not by our works of righteousness which we have done, but according to His mercy He saved us, by the washing of regeneration, and renewing of the Holy Ghost. Which God poured out on us abundantly through Jesus Christ our Saviour (refer. Titus 3:3-6). The reason I wanted to share these scriptures was they show us the promblem first. Then they show the truth and the way. Sometime we need to see the real us. To recieve the promise's of God, and to see the key word that Titus started with was "were". Because when we except Jesus as our Saviour. He begins to regenerate us through the Holy

Spirit. Which will start to produce a new way of life into us as believers in Him. We should not speak any evil about anyone, But we should be gentle and kind to everyone (refer. Titus 3:2). This means never to put people down with harsh words, but lift them up with loving-kindness. This is our mission as a memeber of the Body of Christ. Not saying we are allways going to get it right. But that we need to set it as a goal and strive to achieve it. Just simply try to be better tomorrow than we was today. Because, now being an entrical part of the Body of Christ. We have become followers of Christ. Follower means to "imitate", so we as the body need to commit to doing the work of the Lord. Keeping our life and condut in line with the head of the body, which is Christ Jesus. To stay in line, is to stay in the word, We cannot drift from the word of God to do the things of the world. We cannot choose immoral sex over a wife, or husband (refer. Eph. 5:25). We should run our house hold, not letting our children, by holding our children reasponsable for their conduct, will bring about obedience in our children in a dignified manner (refer 1 Tim. 3:4). We should have love for one, and another, not hating anyone or anything, for love will cover a multitude of sins (refer. 1 Peter 4:8) We must learn to say no, and not be filled with selvish pride, but humble ourselve's before God and others. For God resisteth the proud and gives grace to the humble (refer. 1 Peter 5:5). We cannot put sin of this world before Christ. For Christ had suffered for us in the flesh, so we must arm ourselves likewise with the same mind: for he that had suffered in the flesh has ceased from sin (refer. 1 Peter 4:1). We need to be of a sound mind in unity on one accord praying for one another knowing that we are the Body of Christ. That Jesus hung on that roughed cross to bare our sins in His own body (refer 1 Peter 2:24). That he became a curse for us, for everyone who hangs on a tree is cursed (refer Galatians 3:13). He never even knew sin yet He became sin so that we might be made the righteouness of God in Him (refer. 2 Cor. 5:21). And we are Christ's; and Christ is God's (1 Cor. 3:23) Let others consider us, as a servant to Christ, and stewarts of the hidden truth of God (refer 1 Cor. 4:1). We as the Body of Christ are to take His orders and execute them to the best of our ability. Knowing that we belong to Christ, which makes us a child of Gods. Knowing that He said: I will never foreget or foresake you (refer. Deut. 4:31). And we are complete in Jesus, which is the head of all rule and authority (refer. Colossians 2:10). Paul is saying we have been filled by Jesus to have the spiritual blessings that we need to furthure the Body of Christ lacking nothing. Remembering that we are dead to our sins, and knowing that Jesus made us alive together with Him, and that God has forgiven us of all trespasses. Blotting out the certificate of debt with it decrees that was against us, which was contrary to us, and took it out of the way, nailing it to the cross (refer. Colossians 2:13-14). Just amagen on judgement day we are standing in front of God and He opens a book, and He say's; on Oct. the third at 1:00 pm you lied at 1:05 pm you lied again and He continues on through the book telling us all our sins. Then God say's; how can you pay for this debt? This is when the cross will appear, and Jesus will step in front of us and say Father they are with me. I paid their price in full. Then God opens another book, and it is the Lambs Book of Life where our name is. Where God has written every good thing we done after salvation. He say's; in Jan. the seventh at 3:00 pm you bought a little girl a pair of shoes, at 7:00 pm you visited an elderly Lady at the hospital and I can only imagen the angel's rejoicing as He reads the good that He put in our life. Because we heard His voice, and we obeyed.

We as a memeber of the Body of Christ will allways humble ourselve's, to pray for the sick. So if there is anyone that is sick or they have a disease like cancer or whatever it might be. The first thing for us to do is to go to God by faith with the Lamb of God. Second is to do what God's word say's; Is any sick amoung you? Let him call on the elders of the church; and let them pray over him, anointing him with oil in the name of the Lord: And the prayer of faith shall save the sick, and Lord shall raise him up; and if He have committed sins, they shall be foregiven of him (refer. James 5:14-15). Let's look at how good and faithful God is. He tells us what to do, go to the elder's. Then He tells us how to do it, anoint their head with oil in the name of the Lord. Then He give's us a solution that it will save the sick. Now here is His promise, if they have committed sin's they shall be foregiven of him. When we listen to His instructions and follow them they are going to work. He is a Holy God and His word does not lie. We just have to claim it by faith, and sometime's healing just begins by proclaiming it. Sometimes we have to stand by faith and continue to pray for it. But when we believe it has been done or is going to be done. Jesus said; Ask, and it shall begiven to you (refer Matt. 7:7). One thing we know is that a sickness or a disease is just a name. Like the flue is just a name, cancer is just a name whatever the name maybe. Our Bible tells us every name must bow their knee to the name of Jesus. That at the name of Jesus every knee should bow, of things in heaven, things in earth, and things under the earth (refer. Phil 2:10). There are diseases in the earth and they have been named. It's time, in the name of the Lord. That we claim by His word that cancer bow their knee, and we stand on a rock "Lord" in faith and we pray until that old cancer bow's his knee, or whatever the disease maybe. We cannot give up, but we can start claiming Gods word by faith in the name of Jesus. When we quote scriputure we will have a better chance at anything we do. I have an example: I went to my brothers house, and he runs my mothers pay fishing lake. Well he was make a picture of an older gentleman the man was seventy eight and he had caught a fourty pound shovelhead. My brother started telling me that this man was in the hospital and the doctors said he would only have about three days and he would die. So I asked my brother for his name, and what hospital was he in, and then I wrote it on a little bussiness card. As I was headed back home I began to rub that card and pray. Then when I got home I prayed again, and the Lord asked me to go and pray for this man. Well I taught it was just me, and I told the Lord that I didn't even know this man or his family. But I told the Lord if you want me to go make it as plane as the nose on my face. Well about five minutes later I told my wife that I was going to the hospital, and I grabbed my bible and went. As I was going I began to talk to the Lord saying I think this is just me wanting to lay hands on someone. But I'am going to go by faith, and please send me with the Holy Ghost, because I cannot do this alone. Well when I got there and walk into the room they had the lights out, and there he laid he was not awake. His son and daughteren law, and his nefew was just setting there. So when I came in the room I told them who I was and then I sat my bible on a table and sit next to it. The son watch me sit my bible down and look at about two or three times as they were telling me. That this man was not doing very well at all. They said he had five tummers the size of golf balls in his brain. Then the son looked at me and asked me to pray for him. I said sure lets all stand and join hands. I told them that I was going to join my faith with theirs, and that we would just trust God, and they agreed. So when I prayed for them I quoted God's word. I prayed the prayer of faith from James chapter five verse fifthteen. When I was done we sit back down, and the son had a tear rolling down his cheek, and said: before you came we asked God to send someone like you to pray for my father. Because we don't know anyone we are from Texas. Well I was thinking Lord you are owesome not only did You want me to be here You conformed it. But that is just the kind of God He is. Well I set there for a while and just listen and told them just a little of my fathers testimonie. Then as I was getting ready to leave I told the family that my brother had made a eight by ten picture of that fourty pound shovel head that their father had caught. And that I would bring them one tomorrow if they wanted me too. They said, that they would like that. Well when I got home I call my sister and ask her to put this man on the prayer list at our Church. Well that next morning all the women was going to a thrift store, but when they met, before they would leave they prayed for that man. So when I got back at the hospital the next day. I could not believe the lights were on the man was awake, and as I walked in the door the man was telling the fish story. I said it is no fish tale I have the proof in my hand, and I gave the family the picture. They was all smiling and laughing. The son came straight to me and shaked my hand and told me thanks that the prayer worked. Then he enterduced me to his father, and we talked about fishing. But the whole time I was thinking about fishing with Jesus not for fish, but for men. I set there a good while with the family. The son told me that he didn't think his father was saved, and ask me to pray for his father. So I went next to the hospital bed and I laid my hand on top of his and I ask him if he would like to except Jesus as his Saviour, and he said yes. So then I prayed for this man, and when I was done there was not a dry eye in that room. The man began to thank me about three times, and his son was thanking me too. So when I was getting ready to leave I told them our prayers would be with them and I would call. What happen next is truely God. Because that man that the doctors said was not going to make it three days. On the third day was being released from the hospital to go home. Now don't take me wrong I believe we all need doctors. But I just saying it is only done when God says it is done. Well about two days later I get a phone call and it is my brother he said guest what, and I said no he didn't die, and my brother said no. He is fishing with his son and he just caught another shovelhead. Now all we can say is God you are so faithful and Your mercy endureth forever. Amen. For us to recieve what God has for us, is to know the word of God, which will come from faith. For THE JUST SHALL LIVE BY FAITH (refer. Gal. 3:11). My dear friend lets give Father, Son, and Holy Spirit all the honor and glory, and just pray. Dear Heavenly Father we thank You for Your Son for He never sin yet He became sin just so we might have a chance to be with You. Please never let us loose sight of what Jesus done for us. We praise You for the Holy Spirit who convicts us of our sins with Your loving-kindness. Which endureth's forever and ever, and we are not even worthy for You are holy and pure. You are the soul creator the ruler of the universe. The Almighty Living God the Father of Jesus. You are the Great I'am, and we worship only You. We humble ourselve's at the feet of Jesus and pray for those that are sick and in the hospital. We lift them all up to You and pray for healing. We pray that you would put your hedges up and around them. That Satan cannot pinatrate that You would cover them on every side. That You would use us to bring them hope, by our faith in You. We pray for strength and courage to reach out to them that are hurting. What ever the case maybe, that You send us with the Holy Ghost who comforts and give's us Your wisdom, who leads us on a straight and narrow path, who is allways with us. We pray that this nation will bow it's knee to the name of Jesus. That this Nation which is under God, would come together as one, arm in arm in one faith, which is for the hope of Christ. So that the Son may glorify the Father who rules heaven and earth. We pray for the Heavenly City the new Jerusalem where God will dwell amoung us forever and ever. This is what we long for and pray for. Because You are worthy of all honor and glory, and we praise the Father, Son, and Holy Spirit on high forever, and ever in Jesus' holy name. Amen. Amen.

My dear, dear friend we know how important prayer is in our life, not only is it away to speak to God, but it is also away to express our love from our heart to God for Him and other's. When we truely express our love towards each other. We are planting a seed, which will let our faith grow (refer 2 Thess. 1:3). We are building a bound in the Body of Christ that cannot be broken and other's will know we are of God. Jesus said: A new commandment I give into you, that you love one another; as I have loved you, that you also love one another. By this shall all men know that you are my disciples, if you have love one to another (refer. John 13:34-35). Think of this if we are teaching a little child how to walk or to talk, and when they do it, we get excited and reward them with hugs and kisses. Now think if we listen to what God said; and then we even took it a step further and obeyed, and we loved everyone. How many hugs and kisses do you think we would recieve? Well here is what God said: And it shall come to pass, if we shall listen diligently unto the voice of the Lord thy God, to observe and to do all His commandments which He commands of this day that the Lord thy God will set us on high above all nations of the earth: And all these blessings shall come on us and, overtake us, if we shall listen into the vioce of the Lord thy God. Blessed shall we be in the city, and blessed shalt we be in the field. Blessed shall be our children, and the fruit of our ground, and the fruit of our cattle, the increase of our cattle, and the flocks of our sheep. Blessed shall be our basket and our store. Blessed shall we be when thou comest in, and blessed shall we be when thou goest out. The Lord shall cause our enemies that rise up against us to be defeated before our face: they shall come out against us one way, and flee before us seven ways. The Lord shall command the blessing upon us in our storehouses, and in all that we put our hands unto: and he shall bless us in the land which the Lord thy God give's to us. The Lord shall establish us holy people unto himself, as he has sworn unto us, if we shall keep the commandments of the Lord thy God and walk in his ways. And all people of the earth shall see that we are called by the name of the Lord; and they shall be afraid of us.. And the Lord shall grant us plenty of goods, in the fruit of our body, and in our fruit of our cattle, and in our fruit of our ground, in the land which the Lord promised unto our fathers to give to us, The Lord shall open unto us his good treasure, the heaven to give the rain unto our land in His season, and to bless all the work of our hands: and we shall lend unto many nations, and we shall not borrow. And the Lord shall make us the head, and not the tail; and we shall be above only, and we shall not be beneath; if that we listen unto the commandments of the Lord thy God, which He command of us this day, and are carefully to observe them and to do them: And we shall not turn from any of the words which He commands us this day, to the right hand, or to the left, to go after other gods to serve them. This is what God told His people to do and they would be blessed. Now this would still stand true for us today and it does. But God took it one step further and made a new covenant with us. By the blood shedding of His only begotten Son. And Jesus said: Follow me, and I will make you fishers of men. Blessed are the poor in spirit for theirs is the kingdom of heaven. Blessed are they that mourn: for they shall be comforted. Blessed are the meek: for the shall inherit the land. Blessed are they which do hunger and thirst after righteousness: for they shall be filled. Blessed are the merciful: for they shall obtain mercy. Blessed are the pure in heart: for the shall see God. Blessed are the peacemakers: for the shall be call the sons of God. Blessed are they which are persecuted for righteousness' sake: for theirs are the kingdom of heaven. Blessed are you, when men revile you, persecute you, and shall say all manner of evil against you falsely, for my sake. Rejoice, and be exceeding glad: for great is your reward in heaven: for so persecuted they the prophets which were before you. The only difference from the two covenants is that the old covenant you had to sacarifice animals. The new covenant God sacarifice His Son once for all sin (refer. Heb. 10:12). We know that the things I wrote from the bible was how to be blessed, not to be saved. There is only one way to be saved and His name is Jesus. The truth is God gave us freedom of choice. But when we choose love with faithfulness it equals favor. Favor from God and man. When we try our hardest to be faithful to the Lords commandments. We are showing the Lord how much we truely love Him. To love Him is to know Him, and there is only one way to know Him. That is to study Him by His word. Let's stop for a moment and think about something in our life that we was successful in. We was successful, because we was faithful. We was successful because we enjoyed or loved doing it, or we would just quit. Bottom line is when we can listen to God's instructions, and obey we will be blessed. Blessed is the man that endureth temptation; for when he has been proved, he shall receive the crown of life, which the Lord has promised to them that love Him (refer. James 1:12). God want's us to mature in different situations. Not to run from our promblems, but if they become unbearable to us. God will provide and escape route (refer 1 Cor. 10:13). God's desires that we focus more on Jame's 1:12 than 1 Cor. 10:13. This is so that God might humble us, and that He might prove us, to do Him good in the last of our days. Now the things we have been talking about are how to receive the blessings of God, His instructions to a blessing. We can see in James 1:12 when God gives instructions He also gave a promise. So if we follow the instructions we will receive the promise for He is Holy and pure and cannot lie. What we allways want to remember is during test or temtations is if we don't get them perfect it will be ok. Why because of the God we serve, knew we were going to make mistakes. This is why He gave His only begotten Son (refer. John 3:16). Not to condemn us but to save us (refer. John 3:17). Because God loves us, He created us, and His love for us was very clear the day of Calvary when Jesus died for all our sin's (refer 1 John 3:1). Blessed are we by the blood of the Lamb, for He covers our sins and reconcile's us to God (refer. 2 Cor. 5:18). Which make's us children of Gods, and Jesus want us to go and sin no more, and God knew we were going to slip or fall or make a mistake. That's why He gave us an advocate or intercessor Jesus Christ the righteous. And He is the propitiation for our sins; and not for ours only, but also for the sins of the whole world (refer. 1 John 2:1-2). Even though we have a intercessor in heaven. We should fight the sins of the world daily, and try our best to overcome them one step at a time, one day at a time, being patient and allowing the Lord to work them out of our lives. By the Holy Spirit which He sent to comfort, and to teach us all things (refer. John 14:26). Today we can find comfort in the Holy Spirit when our test and trials come about, if we believe by faith. The only way we can conquer sin is by Christ who lives in us (refer. Gal. 2:20). This is us by faith in Christ, depending on Him for our strength and all of our necessity. When we believe, this is when our heart is filled with peace, joy, and love, that comes from Christ living within us, and it will flow over and into our family, friends, and eventually our co-workers. Being a good example of Christ is not allways what we say, but in our action's in what we do. To be a good example could come from clean language being slow to speak and quick to hear. Could come from being to work or where ever we have to go on time. Could come from helping some one with what ever they maybe doing. Could come from just letting someone else go first. Could come from a kind word when someone else is feeling blue or down in the dumps. Could come from us showing someone else we care and are concerned with their promble's. Could come from our ministry at church. Could come from a number of things. We just don't allways know how the Lord is going to use something we do as simple as a kind word to touch someone's life, but He does. The bottom line for us Christian's today is beawe, and to know if we have truely excepted Christ, our could will turn into would. Because we would do anything for the one we truely love. My friend lets pray together. Dear Heavenly Father thank You for the love You showen us. When You gave us Your only begotten Son. He is the true example of what we need to focus on. We praise only You for You are worthy. You are the ruler, and creator of the universe the Father, Son, and Holy Spirit the trinity. We humble ourselve's to pray for the sick, the homeless, the men, and women of war. We pray that You would give the wisdom and strength to carry out Your plan. For Your will and purpose. For Your Grace and riches. For Your honor and glory. For Your will to be done on earth as it is in heaven. We pray for the kingdom to come. For new Jerusalem, the heavenly city. Blessed be the name of our Lord. Forgive us our debts, as we forgive our debtors. Lead us not into temptation, but deliver us from evil: For Yours is the kingdom, and the power, and the glory, for ever. Please forgive us for we have sin against You. We arc sinners. But now we have choosen Your Son as our Lord of Lords, as our King of Kings, as our Saviour and we pray that You will let our light shine for the world. That You the Almighty would send us with the Holy Spirit as we go out into the world, and turn our could into would. In Jesus' holy name. Amen.

Body of Christ is a symbolic expression for the church. The risen Christ dwells in His body and presides over the church. Which we the members of the body are the church, and our job is to preceive how God's power has change us since salvation. We as christians experience a greater extent of God's divine strength in our daily living. God's power has exalted Jesus' name far above all spiritual creatures. This means God appointed Jesus the head, or the ruler over all thing for the benefit of the church. For the church is His body. Because Jesus' with His wisdom skillfully infused His people with His own life and character. So it is for the good of the church that Christ is the divinely appointed ruler of the universe. For He filled the church with Himself, and the church is the receptacle containing the grace and virtues of God Almighty Himself (refer. Eph. 1:19-23). Christ assigns spiritual gifts to His body to accomplish His work and bring believers to maturity (Eph. 4:7-13). Members of the body are to care for one another. That there should be no division in the body; but that the members should have the same care one for another. And if one member suffer, all the members suffer or one member be honored, all the members rejoice with them. For any church to function properly, every member should do his or her part in a joyful spirit together with the other members (refer. 1 Cor. 12:25-27). This is being a church, which is not the building. It is being a Body of Christ, a gathering of believers for Christian worship (refer.

Acts 15:4). It is a place for the redeemed who belong to Christ Himself (refer Gal. 1:13). For Christ is the head of His body the Church and His will is to be preeminent (refer Col. 1:18). This is saying Jesus should hold first place in a Christians life. This will only happen when we bow to His authority, and we are willing to obey His word, and by us yielding to His Spirit, submitting to His church leaders, doing His will, and by laying our burdens on Him. Now our mission as a Body of Christ or as a Church is to win the lost (refer Luke 4:18). It is also for us to minister to others in the world. For our hope of a glorified body is based on Christ's victory over the grave (refer. Romans 6:6). Now our promise is, as believers we will recieve a glorified body, free of sin and death, at the return of Christ (refer 1 Cor. 15:50-57). The redeemed body that we will have, will be like that of Christ's glorified body (refer. Phil. 3:21). This will be immortal and incorruptible (1 Cor. 15:53-54). This is why the Christians of the Body of Christ should never fear death. Because we are given a new spiritual body for enternity in heaven (refer. 2 Cor. 5:1). This is not my promise to you. This is God promise to us from His word, all we have to do is believe by faith and accept His grace. Which is the Son of God, our messiah, the annointed one, the spottless Lamb, the Lamb of God, our Sheperd, our Lord of Lords, our King of Kings, our Saviour.

Dear friend we all know when the Lord came the first time. He came from His high throne as God to become a man. He humbled Himself and was born in a stable in Bethlehem. He came to save us from the sins of the world, not to condemn us. He came to teach the gospel, to spread the good news. He came to make fishermen of fish, fishermen of men. He came to reconcile us to the ruler of the universe the Almighty Living God, the Great Jehovah – Jireh. He came to die for us, to nail our sins on a cross. Once for all the sins of the world. So that we would have a chance at enternal life with Him. Dear friend that was just a quick version of why He came the first time. But here is what is going to happen the second time He comes, and He is not going to be humble this time. For He is coming riding a white horse (refer Rev. 19:11). The white horse is to repersent victory. His eyes will be as a flame of fire, "this repersents the anger or the wrath of God for the rebellion that will not repent" and on His head are many crowns, "this crown is representing His total sovereignty and authority" and He has a name written, that no man knew, but He Himself (refer. Rev. 19:12). And He will be clothed in a robe dipped in blood: and His name is The Word of God (refer. Rev. 19:13). This presents Christ as the revelation of God Himself. And the armies which were in heaven followed Him upon white horses, clothed in fine linen, white and clean (refer. Rev. 19:14). This is the angels and saints of God which is us and the ones of the old testament. By us riding on white horse's too, this means we are going to share in the victory with Christ, and our bright white linen will represent our righteousness. And out of His mouth is a sharp sword, that with it He shall smite the nations; and He will rule them with a rod of iron: and He treadeth the winepress of the fierceness and wrath of the Almighty God (refer Rev. 19:15). The sword will repersent the judgement that will come from His spoken word. This means Christ will destroy the unbelievers of the nations with the spoken word of God the rebellion will fall, because they would not repent. And He will have on His robe, and on his thigh a name King of Kings, and Lord of Lords (refer. Rev. 19:16). This is to repersent the power Christ has over the universe. He is king over all them who called themselve's kings, and He is Lord over all them who called themselve's lords. And then a angel standing in the sun; will cry out with a loud voice, saying to all the birds of the heavens, come and gather yourselves together unto the supper of the great God (refer. Rev. 19:17). God is calling the birds of the sky to eat the flesh of those who died in the battle of Armageddon. Then the beast, and the kings of the earth, and their armies, gathered together to make war against Jesus and His people or army. The army of the beast and of the kings of the East are going to gather at Armageddon to try to prevent the return of the kingdom of Christ. Jesus will quickly defeat and capture the Beast and the false prophet the one that was doing miracles in his presence and he had decieved them that had recieved the mark of the beast, and them that worshiped his image. These will be the first inhabitants of the lake of fire. And the rest of the kings and armies will be killed by the word of Christ. He will simply just speak the word and they will die (refer Rev. 19:19-21). The unbelieving survivors of this Tribulation. Will then be judged by Christ. Then He will sentence them to the everlasting fire (refer. Matt. 25:41). Then an angel will come down from heaven, having the key to the bottomless pit and a great chain in his hand (refer. Rev. 20:1). The key repersents the authority, the bottomless pit is a place where Satan dwells (refer. Rev. 9:1-2, 11), and the chain repersents imprisonment and binding. And then the angel will grab onto the dragon, that old serpent, which is the Devil, and Satan, and bound him for a thousand years. Casting him into the bottomless pit. Then setting a seal upon him. So that he could not decieve the nations, till the thousand years were up, and after that he must be released for just a moment (refer. Rev. 20:2, 3). The seal repersents the authority of God and guarantee's that satan will not be released for a thousand years.

For this thousand years Satan will not beable to tempt or decieve anyone. During this thousand years any temptations to sin will have to come from within those people who are born after the kingdom begins. Now after the thousand years are completed.

Satan will be released from his prison. Then he will go out to decieve the nations, which are in the four corners of the earth, to gather them togethe to battle. Jesus and His army, who is as many as the sand of the sea (refer. Rev. 20:7, 8) Satan is released from his prison to make one final attempt to defeat Christ. He will go out to decieve the nations into rebellion against the Almight Living God. All this will take place, for this is Gods word and he will not lie. For He is holy and pure, and here is what God is going to do to end the battle. And they went up on the breadth of the earth, and surrounded the camp of the saints, and the beloved city: and fire came down from God out of heaven, and devour them. Then the devil that decieved them was cast into the lake of fire and brimstone, where the beast and the false prophet are, and shall be tourmented day and night for ever and ever (refer. Rev. 20:9, 10). This will be the end of Satan and his henchmen, the Antichrist and the false prophet, and they will be tourmented for enternity.

Now my friend being a member of the Body of Christ. We will develope a dedication to the will of God, but this will come in time. Our dedication will be and act of surrendering to Gods will for our lives. This is when we become a living sacrifice (refer. Romans 12:1). It is our daily dependence in God to transform us to the likeness of His Son, Jesus Christ. When we seek to find the will of God we must also prepare ourselves to commit to doing the will of God, as it is revealed to us by the word of God. We as Christians should allways make every decision that we are faced with. On the basis of biblical principles, knowing our obedience will only bring the blessings of our Lord thy God. Knowing the service of love is to be given to all. Through the grace given into us, to every one that is amoung us, not to think of ourselve's more highly than we ought to think; but to think soberly, according as God has dealt to everyone the measure of faith (refer. Romans

12:3), Love not the world, neither the things that are in the world. If anyone love the world, the love of the Father is not in them (refer. 1 John 2:15) This is simple to us being a member of the Body of Christ. We are to love God first and foremost. We as the Christians of today can depend on the scriptures to defeat the temptations of the world. So lets stand together in unity of the Spirit, in the bond of peace. There is one body, and one Spirit, even as we are called in one hope of our calling; One Lord, one faith, one baptism, one God and Father of all, who is above all, and through all, and in us all (refer. Eph. 4:3-6). So we as the members of the body have placed our trust in Christ for our salvation. Amen

I would like to end this chapter with a testimonie about our Body of Christ. As you all know I have gave a testimonie how a car painter was saved in a garage. Well it was a garage through the week and on Saturday night they would pull out the car's and set up the altar, and stage for the worship team. Well this was our Church for about two seasons. A town ordinance said that we couldn't have Church there no more, because we didn't have the proper rest rooms and a few other details. So our pastor got with another pastor from the next town over. Where we began to have our Church, but we had to wait till one o'clock. Which was ok it was not about the time it was about Jesus. This went on about two more seasons. But while we was there we open a food pantry to give away food in another town. We never lost one member during all of this. It was just the oppisite we gain members, we were baptized, and we all stood in faith believing that God had called us to be a Body of Christ. We now have our own building in the same town that we have our food pantry in. I know that I have shared this before, but I felt lead to share it in this chapter. For turely this is what we all have to do sometimes wether it be in the body or in our life. Sometime we just have to be patient and stand in faith on a rock, and God will grow that body or grow us spiritually, and this will come from our faithfulness to God.